SHUT THE DOOR,

You're Lettin' in the Flies!

J U N E   F U L T O N   E L L I S

*Our mission is to efficiently provide the world's finest, most comprehensive book publishing
service, enabling every author to experience success. To find out how to publish your book,
your way, and have it available worldwide, visit us online at www.trafford.com*

Trafford rev. 7/12/2010

 www.trafford.com

North America & international
toll-free: 1 888 232 4444 (USA & Canada)
phone: 250 383 6864 ♦ fax: 812 355 4082

DEDICATED TO MY BELOVED FAMILY

~~~~~~~~~~~~~~~~~

Dedicated to the memory of father and mother –
Lloyd and Emma Fulton –
and brothers, Jake and Russell

Written with appreciation for so much
input from my brothers and sisters –

Jake, Wade, Barb, Weldon, and Fran

and from cousins – Annabelle, Anita 1,
Anita 2, Bonabeth, and Hazel

also from husband – John

Contents

SHUT THE DOOR
You're Lettin' in the Flies

By June Fulton Ellis

I WAS LYING ON MY BED watching the baby sleep (I loved babysitting him)--Mason, the spittin' image of his father, my nephew Greg. He was so dear, a handsome 8-month-old boy with coal black hair. I thought of my own child, Debbie, a young woman now. She was the beautiful baby girl we waited seven years for and she has brought us such joy, fun and laughter through the years with her special brand of humor. It is a wonderful thing that generations go on. Some of my brothers and sisters are grandparents now--all of the grandchildren have different personalities, and are equally precious. Our family is a very loved and loving, loyal and caring one.

It was springtime, a beautiful day in late April, 2001. My thoughts took me back to my own childhood, back to the big old Fulton farmhouse in Greene County, Missouri. We lived in the Ozark Mountains area in the southwestern part of the state, north of the largest "hills", but we kids didn't know to appreciate its beauty.

We didn't notice when the leaves of the various trees and the sassafras and other bushes turned brilliant, vibrant colors-- all shades of reds, oranges, yellows, browns, etc. We didn't notice with any particular care--even fleetingly--the soft, warm, dusty well-worn paths around our house; we just took them for granted along with the crisp green grass of the lawn they skirted or crisscrossed. We took for granted, too, the comfort of the warm sunshine that caressed us, and didn't give any particular study to the beautiful clear blue skies above us with their fleeting white clouds.

My father's name was Lloyd Lancelot Fulton; he was tall (6'6"or so), blue-eyed and lanky, no fat on him anywhere. He had dark brown hair for most of his years, until he began to gray and grow a little bald later. His nickname was "Long Legs Fulton". He was very quick-witted and he made me laugh a lot. He loved to drink Dr. Pepper cola, which came in 4-oz. glass bottles then, as did other soft drinks.

He had many relatives, almost all farmers, scattered around the local country on farms east and south near Springfield. Very few were within walking distance, but that didn't keep them from visiting in each other's homes. Often, as the years passed, the transportation they used for these visits gradually became more and more comfortable and inviting. AND, of course, they were among the many that helped each other out with the big chores such as hay baling, threshing, silo filling, butchering, etc., bringing wagon teams, pick ups, tools and equipment needed for specific undertakings.

Mama's name was Emily Elizabeth (Braun); almost everybody, family and friends alike, called her Emma for some reason that I never knew. She was about 5'3" tall and was considered to be very pretty, I've heard. For many years when I was too young to know better, I thought that she was 27 years old all of the time, period. I never noticed any differences in her appearance, never counted her years as they passed by.

I've often wondered when and how Dad and Mama met; was it love at first sight? Their farm homes weren't many miles apart. They may have known each other earlier, but someone suggested they may have met at a pie supper at Kinser Elementary School where Dad bought Mama's pie for a high price after haggling with other bidders--his buddies, who were probably laughing as they were running up the bidding on him.

I wonder, too, how long they dated, where and how (buggy? car?) they went on dates, and if they dated many others. It would be interesting to know--was he the wild young man we've heard about from friends and relatives? How so? I can't imagine that he was a quiet, studious type.

What was their wedding like? I have heard they were married January 1, 1925. Was it in a church? Was it in someone's home? Because we have found no pictures of a wedding itself, I believe it wouldn't have been a grand affair. Where did they live when they were first married--the lower place maybe, or on the big home place with Grandma and Grandpa Fulton to help with the farming? I heard also that Uncle Baxter and Aunt Mary Wills stood up for them, and there is one picture of the four of them that our cousin Annabelle thinks may have been taken on their wedding day.

I find it hard to imagine--and regret very much--that in all those years at home with them, I never asked many questions regarding their younger lives or the lives of their parents and other relatives. I can't imagine, either, that they never brought up the subject themselves, nor were such personal things discussed when families got together for Sunday visits, etc., as we do now in a more enlightened society.

I wish now that families then could and would have taken more casual and close-up pictures and written more definitive things down for their future generations. Many of the few pictures I've seen are formal, studio pictures. Most early snapshots that have turned up are cloudy, and facial features are hard to make out; some are cracked and/or badly torn. A few more pictures are showing up since I have put my big family on notice that I am writing this and need any help they can give me.

Neither were there pictures of our neighbors and many friends, something I would so much enjoy seeing, both in their younger years and as they grew older.

Much, much later we did have a small Kodak box camera. Sadly, not many pictures were taken and so many of those that were taken have long since been lost. My brother Weldon recently sent me a very few wonderful--although a little dim, smudged and grainy--black and white pictures of us when we were very young, taken by aunts, uncles, or older cousins, taken outside in our yard or that of a neighbor or relative.

MAMA

MAMA HAD A GENEROUS SOFT lap for cuddling her babies and kids when she sat down, which was infrequently during the daytime because she was always so busy taking care of us all with her cooking, cleaning, laundry, gardening, etc. I don't recall having ever seen her taking a much-needed nap in the daytime, although years later I remember that she had "dizzy spells" on occasion and had to lie down for a while, a miserable something that both Fran and I seem to have inherited.

In spite of her constant working inside our home and out, she had a soft, gentle, loving touch of sympathy in her arms and well-worn hands and a special, soothing, soft cooing sound in her voice to chase away our pain or frustration. I believe she was born to be a very special mother. Her own mother was a sweet, loving person who was always so glad to have us visit and we lost her when we were all very young.

Mama had a fair complexion, blue eyes and dark brown hair. There was a small contrary patch of hair over her left ear that had a mind of its own--it wouldn't stay curled for very long but just stuck almost straight out. I have one very much like it over my left ear. Farm women, in our area at least, didn't color their hair then. She did have a

Marcel curling iron which, when heated on a stove burner, made large, soft waves in her hair. She sometimes let me use it for fun on my short hair, if I promised to be very careful not to burn myself. She later had a pair of eyelash curlers but seldom used them.

Rural women, in our area at least, also didn't wear mascara or eye shadow; anyone who might try it would maybe have been considered to be a "kept woman". Mama had a box of face powder (color Rachel) and she wore just a slight touch of rouge on her cheeks and only the faintest touch of the same rouge on her lips, if any--that was the extent of her makeup. She had small bottles of Taboo and/or Midnight colognes; not every-day stuff for her, she felt.

I also don't remember seeing her look unkempt; her hair was always curled, and she always managed to smell good, no matter what chores she had just finished.

I know that each year took its toll on her looks and interests as the family grew, although it wasn't apparent to us then. Her hands and short nails showed the effects of her never-ending housework, gardening work, etc., and the harsh homemade lye soap she often used. There were no bottles of hand lotion sitting around but she always felt soft to our touch and I do remember seeing a jar of Ponds, Lady Esther or sometimes Jergens face cleansing cream in her room.

There weren't many brands of toothpaste and shampoo available. She must have had her hair permed pretty regularly and kept it curled. There were only a few deodorants to choose from, and sometimes she smelled like talcum powder. A pleasing Christmas gift for her may have been a pretty box of good-smelling body powder.

She had several large cotton aprons to tie around her waist to cover the front bottom half of her dresses--some of them were made with bibs and some were not. She made them from flour sacks or colorful remnants she had on hand or got at the store, some plain, some patterned, all with big pockets. She put a clean one on at the start of each day and it was used in many ways. She turned it up and loaded it with potatoes, snap green beans, peas or other vegetables or fruits she had just picked fresh from her garden when she was hoeing or pulling weeds and didn't take a basket with her.

She used it to shoo flies away; she wiped her hands on it; she gently wiped away a crying baby's tears with it or dirt from a smudged young face. Aprons kept her every-day dresses somewhat cleaner for a short spell; she had many, many aprons in every wash and I remember hanging them by the waistband on the clothes line and ironing them all for many years. Colors were not coordinated then, so dresses and aprons would have matched only by accident.

Her head was covered with a bonnet or one of Dad's old straw hats when she went outside to work or rest. Because of her daily chores she spent many hours outside in the sun and wind. Her arms and lower legs were tanned by the sun but never her face. She wore sturdy oxfords to work in her garden, or sometimes a pair of Dad's old shoes.

It wasn't important to us kids if someone was fat or skinny; there was no reason to notice or wonder about how and why Mama's weight and shape changed every other year or so. She became "fleshy" in her later years but maybe we just didn't notice until then. She kept herself neat and clean through all the years. There were no spas, no aerobics classes, no swimming aerobics and no riding exercise machines. She didn't get out and run down the road at a regular pace; there were no weight loss classes or pre-measured diet food or drink regimens. Her "home" work kept her busy.

When I was a few years older, we didn't always agree on all things, but I understand now that some rebellion by the young is one part of growing up........and, now, I see that she was right MOST of the time. She was such a good mother, loving and pretty patient with seven kids underfoot constantly, sometimes drowning our yelling and fussing with her singing, keeping an ever watchful eye on us.

We were picking up clues about right and wrong from her and Dad without even knowing it. Her life wasn't about her so much as it was about her family and what she could do for us. We knew we could count on her in any kind of trouble.

MAMA, DAD and KIDS

WE LIVED ON THE NORTH (Greene) side of the Greene/Christian County line, a graveled road, and our home faced south. I was born there in November, 1925, the first of seven children. Our births were spaced to one every other year, although I don't think births were especially planned back then! They did the right thing, having a girl first. That meant Mama had help with the younger kids, cooking, cleaning, washing, ironing, etc.--everything oldest daughters were expected to do as soon as they were big enough. I got to be pretty adept at carrying a baby on my scrawny hip, mimicking Mama.

Two brothers were next. John Jacob was born in July, 1927; a year and a half later in December, 1929, the day after Christmas, Charles Wade arrived in their home. Both were born at the "lower place" mentioned later. In a couple of years, it was almost like having twins--they were always together, loud, wrestling, playing, rough-housing and picking on the next child, Barbara Dean, mostly to ruffle my feathers.

It would have been nice to have the brothers separated by the next girl--less wear and tear on Barb and me--but it worked out for the best as far as the chores were concerned, and later after Dad died. Now none of us would change a thing! Barb is Mason's proud grandmother.

Except for three or four years when Jake and Wade were born, we lived in the house our Grandpa John Fulton had built on the front forty (acres) of the "old farm place" in Greene County and the boys started helping with the outside chores at an early age. The third brother arrived there in the summer, at the end of June, 1933--Frank Weldon, a rare light blond in our family, with deep-set eyes. He was born to be constantly adventurous, nosy and seemingly programmed with a zillion questions, set to start with his first words and last throughout his life-- he now has a zillion answers, too, having traveled all over the globe in his work!

A second sister was born in February, 1935, Minnie Frances, kinda blond, delicately pretty, shy and sweet. She resembles Mama's family more than the rest of us do. Fran tried to tag along with Barb and me, with our friends, anywhere and any time we were doing something, but, as most kids do, we thought she was "too little" for us. She and Barb were nearer in age; that meant that I didn't spend as much time with Fran as a child as I wish now I had, although as she grew older, she joined us all in our yard games, etc., and played dolls and paper dolls with Barb and me in the evenings.

Her tear pool has always topped off just below the bottoms of her eyes, evident when she is sentimentally touched, which is often. Barb is not quite so quick to tears, depending upon the reason for them, and I lean to be more like Fran, even worse now for both of us since we've aged. The boys were more stoic and manly, not to be seen crying--wincing a little, maybe, but NO, not crying!

A year and a half later in September, 1937, the last child was born--another brother, Carl Russell, a redhead like Aunt Lydia, always eager to please, and he, too, followed Dad around constantly. Everybody was inclined to spoil this little tag-along just a little bit. As the youngest, he took a lot of loving teasing all the years we had him. He, as we all did, had blue eyes; his went great with his red hair.

Almost all babies born to farm families during those years, unless complications were expected, were born at home with the help of some of our neighbor women that were called mid-wives. They had become very experienced and adept in handling these miracles again and again through the years.

I was much too young then to remember anything about the births of Jake and Wade, but I remember clearly the first time I saw Barb. I was a skinny little almost-six-year-old kid.

I was always being sent down the road to Aunt Ida's house for a while for some reason during the births of my brothers and sisters. When I was allowed to come back home this time, I heard a weird squeaky sound, maybe a baby pig or lamb or such, but why? We didn't take any animals, even cats or dogs, into the house. I searched all over the house for the source of this sound.

I found my mother in bed in the front bedroom where company stayed overnight. Very unusual! Neighbor ladies and aunts stood by the bed, smiling, looking down at Mama, who was holding something wrapped in a small blanket. She turned back a corner of the blanket; there was a tiny, red, wrinkled, crying face, no teeth, tongue wriggling around, eyes closed, all framed by lots of curly black hair. Scrawny little arms had tiny fists clenched, jabbing at the air, and scrawny little legs were kicking at the soft little cotton flannel blanket it was wrapped in. A baby! A girl, they said.

Where did it come from? Did someone bring it? Why was it in this room in bed with Mama? Could we keep it? It was so little! They named her Barbara Dean. I couldn't know then that that baby girl and I would share a bedroom when we grew a few years older. I spent so many hours with her. It was good training for caring for the kids to come later. As I look back at it, that pretty little sister turned out to be the first really big outright joy of my life and made me become more responsible, although I wasn't aware of it at the time. I got to help with her care and protect her from the mischief of those two brothers between us!

Several years later, when she was a first-grader, every day in nice weather I toted her on the seat of my bicycle to Wolf Grade School a mile and a half away on a graveled, most oftentimes rutty, country road. I dreaded passing the white two-story Brazel house where the big Collie dog lived behind the white wooden-stake fence. He barked and barked and rattled me so much that we sometimes fell off the bike and had the skinned knees and dirty skirts to prove it.

Our own dog, Old Pood, the black and white spotted product of several dog breed mixes through the years, was a much sweeter dog; the littlest children could ride on his back and he loved their "wallering" him around in the yard. We also had a few outside cats of every color, age and size that usually slept in the barn. At one time or another we might have to care for an orphan baby bunny, and we hand-fed a motherless lamb or two in the yard.

Dad was considered to be the head of our family, but Mama was the boss of all things in and around the house. There was an unwritten code of honor--no tattling to our parents unless there was danger involved.

Sometimes after a small crime, Mama asked if we wanted a good spanking. Of course, we said yes; crying or pleading one's case was useless. Not knowing what a bad spanking would be, a good spanking was bad enough; it was nice to have a choice. A good spanking was being turned over Mama's lap as she sat in a chair while she used her open hand or a wooden paddle to spank us. Sometimes all of us were in trouble at the same time and we really didn't enjoy watching this procedure. We were sure she had eyes in the back of her head.

If our bad deed warranted it, she used a small, thin switch we ourselves had to break off from a tree limb; it didn't help to pick out the smallest one we could find; any size had a sting in it. Maybe it would be the fly swatter applied to our buttocks or bare legs three or four times to get our undivided attention. It was really more of an attention getter than a punishment, as was the firm tug on an earlobe.

Wade got to be pretty good at gingerly outrunning the hand that was doing the spanking; he laid out almost magically parallel to the ground and ran high stepping around Mama in a wide circle as she held his arm with her other hand, and very few of her "spanks" landed on his body. He had lots of practice and probably could have won this event in a track meet had he had a chance to do so. I don't recall who we rooted for.

If we were precocious enough that it went so far that Mama sent us to Dad for discipline, we knew that was not a good thing, although there was no fear of being hurt. He used the knuckle of his right middle finger for one short attention-getting rap to the top of the head or the threat of "I'll get my belt out!" Hearing that once was enough! No. We never in any way received a beating, but we knew his was the final word on the subject.

"No" was "no", "maybe" was 75% "no". There were also "go ask your Dad" and "go ask your Mama". There was to be no begging, no bargaining, no pouting, whining or wheedling; just go on your way and try another day or just forget about it. We had no negotiating skills. As the oldest, I was almost always the one picked to ask Mama and Dad if we could go someplace or do something; if it worked out to our advantage, I was picked to ask again the next time. I was also held responsible for any damages that may have occurred.

We had local words and phrases such as the following in our vocabulary:

"elt" - same as "well", pronounced with two syllables, indicating a kind of disbelief

"wup" – same as oops, used after a small accident or spill

"do - as in do the dishes, do the laundry, do the milking, etc.

"plack" – play like (we did a lot of this)

"dinner" – noontime meal, now lunch

"supper" – evening meal, now dinner

"tote" – have someone riding on the seat of your bike

"plumb wore out" – tuckered out, tired

"y'all" – you all - seems to be an Ozarkian thing (Mo., Ark., etc,)

"high-fallutin'"– uppity, unlikely

Mama sang to us to put us to sleep, sometimes in German; one song was called "Hi-lee, Hi-lo" but I don't remember the words. She had a lovely soprano voice. One song was, in retrospect, not very beautiful and, I'm sure, wouldn't have the approval of child psychologists today. It was in English and had a beautiful tune, but the words!!

"Oh, don't you remember, a long time ago,
were two little babes, their names I don't know.
Were stolen away, one bright summer day,
and lost in the woods, I've heard people say.
And when it was night, so sad was their plight.
The moon went down and the stars gave no light.

They sat on a log and bitterly cried.
Poor babes in the woods, just laid down and died.
Poor babes in the woods, just laid down and died.
And when they were dead, the robins so red,
brought strawberry leaves and over them spread.
She sang them a song the whole night long.
Poor babes in the woods, now they are gone."

And we were expected to go to sleep?!

Another sad song was:

"May I sleep in your barn tonight, Mister; it is cold lying out on
the ground.
May I sleep in your barn tonight, Mister; I have no other place
to lie down."

Some years later, sung mostly as a round, one of our songs
was:

"School days, school days, dear old golden rule days.
Readin' and writin' and 'rithmetic, taught to the tune of a
hickory stick.
You were my girl in calico, I was your bashful, barefoot beau.
I wrote on your slate 'I love you so', when we were a couple of
kids."

And this one, also a round:

"Whoever stole my big black dog, I wish they'd bring him back.
He chased the big chicks over the fence and the little ones through
the cracks.

The big chicks over the fence; the little chicks through the cracks. Whoever stole my big black dog, I wish they'd bring him back."

Another round:

"Every time I go to town, the boys keep kickin' my dog around. Makes no difference if he is a hound; they'd better quit kickin' my dog around."

Another:

"Reuben, Reuben, I been thinkin', what a great world this would be, If the boys (girls) were all transported, far across the deep blue sea!"

And:

"La-a-azy days, sittin' in the sun.
How you gonna get your day's work done?
La-a-azy days, la-a-azy days, la-a-azy days."

And:

"Oh, where have you been, Billy Boy, Billy Boy?
Oh, where have you been, charming Billy?"
"I have been to seek a wife, she's the joy of my life,
but she's a young thing and cannot leave
her mother."
"Can she bake a cherry pie, Billy Boy, Billy Boy?
Can she bake a cherry pie, charming Billy?"
"She can bake a cherry pie, quick as a cat can wink
its eye,

but she's a young thing and cannot leave her mother." Plus other "can" and "does she" verses.

This one was popular, too: Words and music by Saxie Dowell, copyright 1940 by Santly-Joy-Select Inc.

"Oh, playmate, come out and play with me, and bring your dollies three, climb up my apple tree. Look down my rain barrel, slide down my cellar door, and we'll be jolly friends, forever more."
It was a rainy day, she couldn't come out to play, with tearful eyes and tender sighs, I could hear her say:
"I'm sorry playmate, I cannot play with you, my dollies have the flu, boo-hoo, boo hoo, boo hoo. Can't see your rain barrel, can't slide your cellar door, but we'll be jolly friends, forever more."

I thought my dad was the funniest, most wonderful man in the world; he was so good with us and I loved him without reservation, as I did my mama. Many warm evenings after a hard day's work doing farm things he tried to relax in the soft grass in the shade of a tree in the front yard; he would lie on his stomach and let the littlest kids walk and roll on his long back; he said it felt good as long as there were no more than two at once and there was no jumping, "rasslin" or knee "jabbin". He sometimes had kids hanging all over him when he sat in a rocking chair and they followed him or walked with him wherever he went. He watched me from the corners of his eyes; he knew I'd laugh at his jokes and sly remarks--and he WAS funny.

We lived in a world where love was a given; we knew discipline and spankings were for our own good--our parents told us so!

Occasionally Dad came home a little too happy with a big grin spread across his face, smelling like at least one bottle of booze, maybe more; maybe it was a fun time with Uncle Wayne at the "men only" pool hall in Springfield. Dad was never a "mean drunk", he was a funny drunk. He joked around with us and played our games with us. There was that special twinkle in his eyes as he teased me. He didn't bring liquor into our home but had it hidden away or bought it later for silo fillings, thrashings, etc. He usually brought us candy or each a small toy in these instances, and Russ was usually the first one to greet him--and sometimes got his own little sack of candy for it.

Mama was so mad at him one time that she wouldn't let him in the house when he got home; she told me to walk with him up and down the road for a while to help sober him up. She just didn't think it was funny. Another time she loaded up all seven of us kids in the pickup to drive us to Aunt Sophie's house. We were scared; we didn't have any idea what was going on. Luckily, she got down the road a piece and changed her mind, but I think she made her point. (He gave up completely his drinking fun when I was about fifteen or sixteen.)

When I got to be about thirteen, Dad and Mama would leave for a while and put me in charge--babysitting, they call it now and pay for it. Sometimes, as soon as they left, we started making fudge, ate it all, and thought we did a good job of cleaning up after, but...maybe we missed washing the "testing" spoon mess made by putting the spoon back on top of the stove, which left a little sweet brown drop that was a dead giveaway, or maybe something else just as careless, such as a smudge on a face. Seven kids cleaning up just called for leaving some little tell-tale clues.

I remember feeling very grownup. I was the boss, sitting in the living room in Dad's big padded wooden rocking chair with my book--although I got little to no respect. The other kids didn't seem to get it, or they didn't seem to care, that I was the boss for the time being. I got very little reading done (sometimes I noticed I was holding the book upside down), rocking ever more vigorously, singing and humming louder and louder to drown out the noises, which got louder and louder, more and more rambunctious, and closer and closer to my chair and my rigid body.

It was mostly Jake and Wade, being boy-onery as was their wont most of the time. They knocked my book to the floor, they hit me with bed pillows, held tea towels over my head down over my eyes. They tipped my chair back and forth, and gave me little "love pats" or pinches. I was a very, very nice, composed and ladylike boss for a very long time; my humming and singing turned into loud then louder songs but those pesky boys finally got to me. I jumped up out of my chair and tore into them--just what they wanted; I'm sure I always got the better of them.

When we saw the truck lights and heard the sound of tires on the gravel in our driveway, we immediately stopped all that activity and settled into our places as if nothing had happened. Chairs were set back in their places, pillows returned to the bedrooms, and dropped items were picked up. Even the babies stopped crying.

About that age, too, or a little later, I got to be a little sassy; Mama said I was a "sassbox". After all, though, I was out in the world, learning lots of new things, and thought I was pretty smart. She said it was more like "smart alec". I remember when my daughter, Debbie, went through the same thing at about the same age. When she didn't get her way, she looked at me through slitted eyes, gritting her teeth and biting her tongue, glaring at me, red-faced. It was all I could do to keep from laughing, because it took me smack-back to my own childhood.

I was gone from home when Barb and Fran would have gone through this rebellious stage with Mama. It had nothing to do with loving her or disrespecting her. I don't know if the boys went through something similar or not with her or Dad. All of us certainly turned out fine in the long run because of this firm discipline, as did our friends and cousins.

We were taught at an early age to be polite to our elders; we were to speak respectfully to them as they arrived on our scene and ask if we could do something for them. We were taught to get up at once and give our seats to grownups, a courtesy that is not regularly being taught these days, it seems.

When one of us kids was praised a little bit for something done really well or for something outstanding and was pretty proud of it, we others chanted "big head, big head" at him. We have talked about it now, and don't remember any excessive praise we ever got from our parents about any of our accomplishments. We, as were our friends and relatives, were expected to do our best, always. Back then, unlike what is done these days, parents didn't go around bragging, hugging, kissing, and saying "I love you" all the time but we knew they did love us. Hugs, kisses and pats were mostly given out with sympathy for hurts, cuts, scratches, bruises, bad colds, etc.--any kind of misery.

We had few, if any, worries. Mama and Dad loved us; they took care of our needs, fed us and cared for us in times of illness or accidents. They saw to it that we were honest, kind and unselfish. Our education was automatic, although very limited by today's standards. We lived life on the farm accepting what we had in terms of family, friends and freedom. I can't think of a time when we were jealous of our friends' or relatives' good fortune, if any. Our personal possessions were about the same as theirs. It was a subject we never even thought about. Crime was never an issue. It was a good time to be a child on the farm.

Mason stretched and opened his eyes; he was just about to start crying when I reached out and reassured him. I picked him up and carried him into the living room. Well, so much for recalling one's life. At least I knew the girl I had been was still there, in wonderful memories. I could and would bring back these and many other memories at any time I wanted to call them back. Sadly, Mama and Dad and their generation are no longer around to share them, but this girl hasn't gone anywhere; I have just grown older and wiser and more appreciative and experienced. AND my family hasn't gone anywhere either. They have just added more family; I held this addition tightly against me and smiled.

OUR HOME

Our house, built in the late 1890s in Greene County by Grandpa John Fulton for his large family, was two stories tall, painted white, and had a black asphalt shingle roof. There were three bedrooms and an attic upstairs. A few years ago, our cousin, Aunt Beulah's son Jerry Cowan, gave each of us kids an 8"x10" front-view picture of the house (in black and white, and seemingly taken in the front/side yard, by a professional photographer on a dark, dreary day) when it was brand spanking new and very plain looking. There had been no landscaping done yet; the yard would be considerably prettier later.

The people in the picture, Dad's family, were dressed up-- the men in white shirts, dark suits and ties, women and girls in long Sunday-best fancy white or pastel dresses with high necklines, long sleeves, full skirts and belted-in waistlines. Some children were looking out of the window from an upstairs front bedroom. The people looked pleasant but very serious and were not smiling ear to ear as is expected of us now. Most persons were standing or sitting at least two to four feet from another person.

No family pictures were taken inside the homes, which would have shown their furniture, décor, etc. Some homes in town had large, ornately framed pictures of long-gone ancestors, dressed in dark, formal clothes, hanging on their walls. I don't recall that we had any of these.

Just a stone's throw away to the west on the Christian County side of that county line road in front of our home was where Uncle Wayne and Aunt Ida Scott (Grandpa John's sister) lived. They and our family were very close, dependent upon each other for many every-day living needs and sharing personal good and/or bad news.

In later years, their daughter Annabelle had grown up and married Bert Whobrey; they and their kids lived just down the road further west past the hollow. Bert was standing near his concrete silo one day when it was struck by lightning; he was unharmed although he was a dab shook up.

There were three tall lightning rods installed later on the roof of our house. Weldon recently sent me some pictures taken several years later during late spring or summer, showing the many tall oak, maple, and walnut trees and the mulberry tree, among others, along with the shrubs, bushes and flowers that had been planted in our yard through the years.

We did not have "patios" then; our front yard was our outdoor living room and playground. We did not eat out there except for big family picnics. Everywhere you might look, kids were playing outside most of the time, in any kind of weather. We had so many games appropriate to any season.

There were no basements under the houses in our part of the country. Almost every home had a grass-covered, mounded-dirt, multi-purpose cellar, more than half-buried out some place close-by in the yard, with rock or wooden plank steps leading down through wooden doors, no lighting. They were storm cellars, large enough to hold several people. They also held the home-canned food on shelves along with the baskets of newly harvested potatoes, apples and anything else that needed to be stored in a cool place.

The cellars faced away from the southwest, as most storms came from that direction, and were skewed a little away from the cold, winter winds blowing fiercely from the north. Rather than being an outside cellar, ours was dug under a corner of the smokehouse floor with rock steps leading down into it from inside the smokehouse itself. It had wooden plank walls and a gravel floor. It most certainly had its own musty smell and damp feel! Some had double doors leading down from the outside into cellars under an outside building nearby.

On the north or back side of the main house, there was a one-story section the width of the house; it had a large attic room over it. The dining room, kitchen, and pantry were included in this section.

There was a raised screened-in porch on the east side of this section; it had a concrete floor and a two-feet-high gray, sculptured concrete block wall running the length of the porch on the east side and on the shorter north wall. It was furnished with a large, rectangular wooden table and many unmatched chairs--many of them slatted wooden rockers, some with slightly padded cushions. The table was a landing place for many things brought inside from the garden, yard, store, school, etc.

This block wall included what was possibly the busiest screen door ever made; all screens themselves were black. It was patched over and over again because of holes somehow having been "accidentally" punched into it over and over again by the kids, and immediately needed to be patched again and probably re-hung or replaced. Window screens in the boys' room suffered the same fate.

Mama had a hard time keeping up with the flies we let inside. There were many screen flyswatters handy wherever we were in the house, but we had not heard of any insecticides for indoor use against bugs of any kind. Big long strips of black gooey, sticky paper were hung outside from eaves and tree limbs to catch insects. Spiders and their webs were everywhere outside, and some were in the house occasionally, but Mama kept after them constantly. Mousetraps were about it for indoor defense against small critters of any kind and we did see a mouse or two on occasion. Maybe our constant running, yelling and scuffling scared them away.

There was a built-in, room-wide, waist-high, wooden, linoleum-topped cabinet on the north end of the porch. We used a long narrow aluminum bucket on a rope pulley to draw up from 150+ feet down cold, clear drinking water from an aluminum-sleeved deep well under that cabinet. This drinking water was kept handy on top of the cabinet in a two-gallon aluminum bucket with a long-handled aluminum dipper in it--everyone drank from the same dipper. Imagine! No ice, no little throw-away paper or plastic cups or glasses. We lived through that and through using the same bath towels many times, too!! The towel was usually pretty wet by the time it got to me.

Mama had some great do or don't commands for using that porch and other rooms. She very often said, in a voice loud enough to be heard by all, louder than our laughing and yelling:

"Shut that door, you're lettin' in the flies."
"Don't slam the door!"
"Don't bring that thing in here!"
"If you're gonna do that, go outside!"
"Quit hittin' your sister!"
"Do you want a good spankin'?"
"Don't talk dirty; do you want your mouth washed out with soap?"
"Don't sass me, young lady!"
"Go wash those dirty hands."
"How many times do I have to tell you?!" and
"Wipe your feet outside!"   (Wipe? On what?)

There were doors into the living room, dining room and kitchen from this porch. Each door had a window in the upper half. Windows themselves throughout the house were double-paned--upper and lower; there were no picture or crank-out windows yet. Outside windows were screened, had very little draping--nothing heavy, maybe sheer curtains with some lace--and had dark green pull-down roller shades used to shut out the hot sun and cold winds. As time passed, Mama did update the sun-baked curtains occasionally. Except for the kitchen, all woodwork was painted with dark walnut varnish.

We didn't worry about window peepers or anyone's seeing in. Only in the wintertime or during storms were the doors closed, never locked! There wasn't a key to be found anywhere; in all the years I lived there, I never saw a key. There was little to no violence; I cannot remember any robberies back then in our rural areas. There was no "what's yours is mine" attitude; things borrowed were returned shortly. Women didn't cuss or talk dirty and men kept outside whatever cussing they felt they had to do. Neighbors looked out for their neighbors. Still, Mama kept an eye on us constantly.

We always came in the back door, through the porch and into the kitchen. In the wintertime, after playing outside or walking home from school through the snow-covered fields, we hung our wet clothing on a double row of wooden hooks on the walls behind the kitchen doors; I don't recall a coat rack anywhere. Most of the time our rubber boots were left on the porch; they were very cold the next morning and we tried warming them by the stove; sometimes the moisture was frozen on their outsides. On other occasions, they might be hung over the knobs at the top of each dining room chair. A family this size would have created quite a lot of wet smelly woolen clothing! I can't imagine it was dry by morning many of those times and there were no clothes dryers.

ENTER OUR FRONT DOOR

ON THE SOUTHEAST CORNER OF the home was a raised front porch with square pillars and a two-feet-high wall made of the same gray sculptured concrete blocks as those used for the wall of the back porch. There were several matching wooden rockers there. This was meant to be the main entrance to the home but was seldom used for that purpose; visitors came to the back porch, as they did at almost all of the homes around.

There were two doors on adjoining right-angle walls of the front porch, both with plain glass window panes in their upper halves.

One led into the middle of the house through a long front hall with its oak floor, where the big, tall walnut telephone box hung on the east wall, with its crank handle on one side and its black metal mouthpiece on the front. We were on a multi-party line; most of the "parties" were neighbors and relatives. We kids were not to use it without permission. Each family had its own ring; ours was two longs and a short. It was hard to get a line out. Everyone would occasionally listen in on calls to everybody else, commenting and laughing with others on the line--maybe the real reason it was called "party line".

From that hall there was a windowed door on the right into the living room on the east where we spent most of our evenings, and another into the parlor on the west. A long stairway led to the upstairs rooms and there was a regular door into the dining room at the end of the hall. The living room had its own wood-burning stove, a few wooden rockers (some kid-sized), a sofa and other chairs and some tables for games, etc. It had, on top of linoleum flooring, a large, patterned, woolen rug that required beating, and there were a few nondescript pictures on the walls.

Pictures were hung centered high on the walls of the rooms, no groupings, usually one large picture of scenery or flowers framed in dark wood, no matter that they were hanging against busy-patterned floral wall paper. Any photographs, always black and white, that were taken by family or friends were usually kept in no specific order in a large cardboard box. Only occasionally was there a big dark leather picture album.

Each year one new large calendar could perhaps be found hanging on a kitchen wall, advertising from a farm machinery company or such that wanted Dad to remember them each day. Maybe there would be one picture on it--cows, horses, a big bull with long horns, or a herd of sheep; it might be a big red barn with silos, possibly a field of corn or a car, truck, or tractor advertisement. With any luck, it would be a stand of trees beside a rushing stream.

The west door on the front porch opened directly into the formal parlor on the southwest corner of the house. Leaving the windows closed in that room helped to keep it cleaner and neater. The kids were not allowed to go in there except for me to clean, which was mostly dusting. When I was a little older, I taught myself to dance in that parlor, to the swing music of the times being played on a small box-like battery-run radio.

This off-limits room was furnished with a beautiful, dark mahogany sofa that was covered in a floral-patterned, dark velvet upholstery material, so soft to the touch. The end sections were made of decorative woven 1"- 1-1/2" wide rattan strips, varnished to match the mahogany arms above them. Across the room from it were two matching upholstered companion chairs with a big square mahogany chest/table between them; I don't recall what it held.

There was a dark, shiny mahogany library table standing against the south wall. On its top was a long, narrow cream-colored lace cloth that hung down over each end of the table, its tassels touching the floor, and, among other things, it held a lovely cream colored, tall decorative kerosene lamp. The room had a floral-patterned dark woolen rug and lace curtains. I don't remember the other furniture, pictures, lamps or wallpaper, but there was another of the hanging carbide ceiling chandeliers with multiple small mantles.

Barb told me that when they were a little older, the kids were allowed to play with their toys in that room. She said the carpet had begun to fade pretty badly and Mama let them color in with crayons the little painted flowers that were printed inside the small squares of the pattern, which she said really worked well for a time.

I have no idea what happened to any or all of this furniture. I can't remember a time when there was a big entertainment event in that room. I remember it was there for Dad's funeral viewing and until Mama moved. She did not take it with her to the little remodeled house down the road. Maybe she sold it when she moved, or maybe it wasn't in very good condition, after its many years of existence, and she had to dispose of it.

A square double archway led from that parlor into a room that was meant originally to be a formal dining room (too many kids for that!) Our family and neighbors didn't entertain like that anyway. Of necessity, Barb and I took it over for our bedroom; we could giggle and talk to our hearts' content there.

SLEEPING, BATHING ARRANGEMENTS

THERE WERE TWO SMALL FIRST floor bedrooms on the west side of this part of the home, one of which had a door into the next bedroom. While there were just a few babies, Mama slept in one of the small rooms with the youngest nursing baby and Dad slept in the other with the next youngest child; evidently they got together sometime. In those days babies were breastfed--no such thing as bottles of formula. If a new mother couldn't nurse her baby for some reason, babies were given small bottles of warmed whole milk. Mama didn't have that problem. On occasion, another woman who was nursing a new baby sometimes filled in.

Eventually, after the youngest nursing baby (Russ) was old enough, the younger kids had one of the rooms; there was the ever-present crib for many years. As the family grew, it was necessary that Jake and Wade move upstairs into their own room.

We did not have innerspring mattresses; we had thin full-size cotton mattresses that rested on top of metal coil springs placed on wooden slats that spanned the space between the bed side-rails; on top of those mattresses we had homemade feather ticks. Sheets (always white) weren't fitted but they were large enough to tuck in around and under both the feather ticks and mattresses; they didn't always end up there.

There were no top sheets; we slept under pretty, well-worn quilts pieced from Mama's sewing remnants; we kids liked to look for the pieces she used from leftovers of our dresses, shirts, etc. The quilts were then filled, lined and quilted by Mama, and they were washed very often.

Mama's commands here (all too often ignored) were "make up your beds!", "don't jump on the beds!" and "no pillow fighting!" There were no "dust ruffles" atop the springs, just a collection of dust balls under the beds until Mama's fussing made us clean them out occasionally.

Winter blankets were heavy woolen. Hand-made quilts were either woolen or cotton, lined sometimes with flannel, depending upon the season they would serve. They, too, were made from the remnants of Mama's sewing on her Singer treadle sewing machine. They also served as bedspreads. Bed clothes, table cloths, and linens were stored in a large double chest of drawers that stood against the wall in the hall.

We had small closets and chests of drawers in the bedrooms; we didn't have many changes of clothes to put in them, mostly pajamas, underpants and socks, and heavy underwear in the wintertime. In the 30's and 40's during and just after the great depression, in rural America most people were very poor by today's standards. We did not have large winter and summer wardrobes. What few shoes we had were scattered over the bottoms of the closets. Our bedrooms weren't always the neatest.

We had no matched bath towel sets and no matched sheet sets, and most of our pillow cases were beautifully hand-embroidered. Sheets and pillow cases, table cloths and other "linens" were stored in a large chest of drawers in the dining room. Pillows had been made by Mama, using duck down and feathers, or possibly wool from the last shearing of the sheep, stuffed inside cotton sheeting.

We used the water hose for kids' summertime baths outside. In the wintertime, a big galvanized washtub was placed next to the wood-burning iron stove in the dining room. Firewood, which had been cut into proper lengths in the spring from the trees in our forests, was dried out during the summer in the back yard near the outhouse. When the weather turned cold, the wood was carried to the back porch and kept dry in a pile there to be added to the fire in the dining room and living room stoves as needed.

Usually each Saturday evening, we kids took turns in the tub, one after another, hot water added as needed. Russell, as the youngest, usually got his tub-bath first; it depended upon who might be the very dirtiest to be last, using the last of the hot water. One side of the body got to be almost too hot for comfort, temporarily stinging and turning red, but the side away from the stove was very, very cold with goose pimples. That was the only time the house really felt cold in the living areas.

We did not have conditioners for our hair; there was a lot of crying, hollering and fussing when Mama tried to comb out the snarls and tangles. The sun and wind were our hair dryers. Our hair was worn too short for braids or pony-tails and it was cut by Mama in our early years, both boys' and girls'. Barb's brown hair was the darkest, Fran's was the lightest, and mine was a mucklededun color. We had the same haircut, fashioned by Mama. Lovely! At least Barb had some natural curl in her hair; Fran and I had both been dealt straight hair. Jake and Wade had brown hair, Weldon was curly blond, and then there was "Red Russell".

When I was a little older, Dad gave me his empty Prince Albert tobacco tins. After cutting off the top and bottom ends, I flattened the tin and cut it with Mama's scissors into 1/4" strips, wrapped them in paper and used them for hair rollers, turning the ends back in over my rolled-up hair to hold them in place. Before that, my hair was worn plain, cut straight around my head just at the level near the bottoms of my ears, with straight bangs cut just above my eyes.

After those Saturday night baths, we put on our long warm flannel pajamas Mama had made for us, some with feet, and wrapped a warmed flannel blanket around ourselves just before running on the cold linoleum or wooden floors to our unheated bedrooms and our fluffy soft feather ticks. As long as we snuggled down in them and didn't move around too much, we were warm and cozy. Sometimes we slept under the ticks for more warmth in really frigid weather.

It was good, peaceful sleeping. Next morning, we awoke with a mound of frost near our noses from our breathing on the blankets. We made a fast run to the nearest warm stove which had been "banked" for the night and fired up again in the morning. There were no indoor bathrooms then; we had small metal pails under our beds to be used on the coldest, snowiest nights, if necessary, which was very rare. Many years later, after Dad was gone and Jake and Wade had moved on, the second little bedroom, after all those years, was made into a much appreciated bathroom.

When the wind was blowing and howling outside in the wintertime, we could hear it whining at the windows trying its best to get inside; the thin, floppy, wire screens rattled back and forth against the windowpanes. The trees, having lost the leaves that had shielded us from the direct heat of the sun in the summertime, gave us no protection now; small limbs scratched against the screens and the outside walls of the house.

The window panes were iced over both inside and outside on most winter mornings, sometimes with fancy patterns made by Jack Frost, and we couldn't see out through them. Sometimes we wrote our names or messages or drew frosty pictures on them with our fingertips. We got used to it. We knew nothing of storm windows. Deep white snow piled up on top of the house roof until the sun melted it enough for it to slide off with a loud crunchy noise.

SECOND FLOOR – SLEEPING

When I started my teens, Mama let me move into one of the three bedrooms upstairs. Jake and Wade had had the southeast bedroom up there for many years and it was always a mess. They made a lot of noise with their toys and yelling and wrestling around.

After perusing a few catalogs for ideas, I decorated it as my 4-H Club project that year. Mama bought me a new unpainted pine dressing table with a curved shape and a matching stool. I made pretty, ruffled, bright, flower-print covers for them and a simple matching bedspread, curtains and pillows. I put up some pictures I found at the dime store. I had a matched brush, hand mirror and comb set for my newly-varnished dresser top and a round mirror above it. As I grew older, I began to accumulate a few more clothes for my closet.

I loved that room and lived there until I left for college! The scenery from the window was lovely; I looked out into trees and down on the yard, bushes, flowers, the grape arbor and the blackberry patch, and past that, a field where the horses, mules and other animals ran free within the boundaries of the surrounding fences. Fran moved in with Barb.

MY OWN LIBRARY!

THERE WAS AN ADDITIONAL BEDROOM upstairs; it had no furniture except a dark mahogany upright piano that was there during my earliest years. I have no idea what happened to it; I think one of the aunts probably ended up with it, which, as far as I know, was her right. It was of little interest to us kids at the time, anyway, and neither Mama nor Dad had any idea of how to play it nor a burning inclination to learn to do so.

Hundreds of books of all sizes and subjects, most of them with bright colorful jackets, were strewn about, a wonderful dusty treasure covering the floor in that room; there was no shelving; there was no order of any kind to the piles. The books were all in good condition, many of them new or near-new. I have no idea why they were there, where they came from or who put them there. I didn't care. I was just so happy they were there and I did take some time to dust and pile many of them together by subject; oftentimes I sat with several on my lap at the same time, enjoying the pictures, written words and the musty smell. I would have cared if someone had taken them away!

I spent many, many hours sitting on the wooden floor in the midst of "my own" library books during my early years, learning about history, math, grammar, spelling and geography—nothing about philosophy, opera, great literature, etc. I read romantic novels and beautifully illustrated religious story books. I read fact and fiction about sea sagas, wars, pirates, soldiers, etc. Later, I would draw on a lined school tablet pictures of big ships with many huge white sails flying in an imaginary wind on rough, stormy seas.

There were children's books such as "The Bobsey Twins", "Little Women", "Nancy Drew" and westerns with their cowboys and Indians and mounted cavalry. There was a variety of books about ways of life I could never have imagined on my own, from pilgrims and their Indian relationships, to royalty and everything in between. Love stories ended with sweet romantic scenes--no nudity, no smut, nothing crude.

I sincerely believe this experience helped me with my grammar, spelling and geography in later years. I was also very much fascinated by the dictionary, and the small globe I found. Subconsciously, I slowly became more and more aware that there was a big world out there (some of it wonderful, some of it full of pain and evil). I found it was full of people different from my own beloved, close-knit little farm family and friends--good people, evil people, crazy people, rich and poor people, slaves and their "masters", and royalty (which I never accepted as right). I hurt for the people I read about that were repeatedly beaten, wrongfully imprisoned, forced to do horrible things, and even killed.

When Jake was about 11, Wade around 9-10, and Weldon about 6 years old, they went into the closet of that room and found Dad's few souvenirs from World War I when he served in France. There were two military helmets. One was an English helmet and one was a German helmet. There was a small metal mirror and a gas mask complete with canister.

There were two swords, both in their cases. Weldon tells me that one was a French bayonet about 2 feet long; the other was a saber sword, curved and long. Dad had also brought home a few empty high-power shell casings and Jake got a spanking from the teacher for taking them to school in his pocket and showing them around. There were a few foreign coins.

They found Dad's old aluminum fold-up Army mess kit there, approximately 5"x 9", and 2" deep, with a metal latch that folded over the attached lid which, when it was unfolded, served as a skillet handle. He allowed us kids to eat from this kit occasionally after that.

We also played with the other things; we have no idea now what happened to any or all of these things and we wish we had them now. There were a few pieces of his drab Army uniform and we later found an old formal picture of him dressed in it and thought him to be very handsome. He never told us any stories about his time in the service in France and we weren't old enough to know what to ask.

KITCHEN, HEART OF THE HOME

I CAN CLOSE MY EYES AND see the rooms. Our kitchen was located in the middle part on the north side of the first floor area. The kitchen and other rooms were papered by Mama and some of the relatives or by helpful neighbor exchange. They had patterned wallpaper, mostly florals, but sometimes checks or stripes, all with wide, pretty borders at the top. The kitchen cabinets were located on the north wall and were painted a just-off-white color. The kitchen, dining and living rooms had small-patterned linoleum flooring. Décor fit for Better Homes and Gardens? Nope.

Growing up, I had a hard time with the upper kitchen cabinets; I don't have any idea how many times I hit my head on their sharp corners, which always resulted in a big bump that hurt considerably and required a lot of rubbing! I could choose between cussing and crying--of course, knowing Mama, I chose crying....partly, too, because my cuss words were few and far between, not nearly strong enough for the pain!

"Doing" the dishes in the sink was more fun and took a lot longer time to do when Barb and Fran grew up enough that we girls could sing as a trio, and we considered ourselves to be quite good at harmonizing and dancing around, a good excuse for the boys to go outside and play.

We had cold running water in the kitchen sink. Water for dishwashing, laundry and baths had to be heated in big kettles on the kitchen stove or on the iron wood-burning dining room stove. In the summertime the big, black kettle outside was used for heating water, or the sun warmed it in buckets placed outside.

Many of our dishes and glasses came in our feed sacks of flour. Some were plain, some were patterned--plaids, checks, birds, flowers, etc. It wasn't noticed they were not a matched set; we didn't even know and wouldn't have cared that dishes came in matched sets! They were bound to be chipped and broken often with so many kids around.

Our "silverware" wasn't silver and not many pieces of it were matched, either. Some of it came in flour sacks, too. From time to time Mama picked up from the dime store whatever pieces of silverware or dishes were needed. Serving bowls and platters, of necessity, were large.

We didn't often have orange juice. Mama sometimes made and canned tomato juice, but there were no small juice glasses; there were no cocktail or wine glasses, either. We never heard of a cocktail. We did have a few small aluminum collapsible drinking glasses for our lunch buckets. This was long before plastic was introduced for household and general use.

On the left side, under the linoleum cabinet top which ran the length of the north wall of the kitchen, was a large aluminum-lined drawer that pulled out from the top into a vee shape; there was a pull-out bread board above that. The drawer held the flour we had the miller grind and sack from our own wheat. Also kept in there was the blue granite bowl holding leftover flour, which was still hollowed out where the big dough-ball had been removed, ready when needed to start a new batch of baking powder biscuits. In the corner of the cabinet top above it was an earthenware crock that held the clabber milk used to make them.

Off the west side of the kitchen was a small walk-in pantry with so many good things on its shelves: sugar, salt, all kinds of seasonings. A slice of fresh apple was put in the jar of rock-hard brown sugar kept there to keep it soft. The one item that was visited most frequently by the kids, especially after school hours, was the huge peanut butter jar. Peanut butter was not homogenized then; we kept a big spoon nearby on the shelf to stir it until it was smooth, then we stuck the spoon or a finger in and took out a big swoosh of it; needless to say the jar was emptied very quickly. Sanitary? What germs?

Terry kitchen towels and many big white square cotton tea towels Mama made from plain flour sacks, hemmed, and embroidered with flower, fruit and bird patterns, were kept in one of the kitchen cabinet drawers. Kept there also were homemade pot holders. Paper towels, napkins, Kleenex, plastic baggies, plastic pot scrubbers, etc.? Never heard of 'em! We did have aluminum foil, though.

We did not have wood-burning kitchen ranges in our home. Our large four-burner stoves, updated a few times, used kerosene for fuel, the burners and oven to be lighted with a match. All had ovens on one side of the stovetop. When I think back to all the food that was prepared there, I can't believe that stove was large enough. Mama had at least three large cast iron skillets and many roasters, pots and pans in several sizes. At mealtime, something was cooking on all four burners and there were maybe a couple of things in the oven. Some of these stoves had small warming cubicles at the top rear. Outdoor cooking on a grill was not yet the "in" thing.

Leftover food, if any, was taken outside and fed to our dog, Old Pood, so there was no need for storage bowls, and no place to put them in the icebox. No one had heard of dishwashers and built-in garbage disposals, besides the fact that there was no electricity. Ice boxes and gas refrigerators had very little space inside them, little more than enough to store milk, eggs (we had fresh ones every day anyway) and butter, and the styles changed often with new inventions.

There were no electric mixers, crock pots, coffee pots, grinders, knives, etc.; things like these were of a large bulky size and were hand operated. Dad sharpened the butcher and paring knives on a pumice stone.

Neither were there any electric vacuum cleaners--we shook rugs outside or hung them on the clothesline and beat them vigorously with the broom or a rug-beater. We used straw brooms, cotton cord mops and dust cloths torn from scraps of old sheets, towels, etc. for cleaning.

For many of the things we bought we received S&H green stamps, and pasted them into the blank books provided;

when the books were full, we could redeem them for merchandise.

Every day Dad put some of the hot water from the tea kettle into his round shaving mug with the round soap in it and swirled his shaving brush around until it was full of thick suds, then spread the suds onto his face. The razor blade folded out from a long narrow slit recessed inside the handle-cover of his razor, which protected both the blade and those using it, and provided him a handle with which to hold the razor steady. He swished the blade around in a bowl of warm water after each stroke.

Before shaving each day, he sharpened his razor on a thick 1-1/2" x 15" leather strop with a metal ring at one end which he hung on a big nail at the end of the upper cabinet near the kitchen sink. He ran his long straight-edge razor blade back and forth against the strop several times until the blade was sharp enough to suit him. After shaving, he cleaned everything up in the sink and put it all away in its special spot in the cabinet, ready for the next day. His dark hair, as was that of the kids, was cut by Mama.

There was a built-in cabinet with shelves in the wall between the kitchen and dining room to hold the dishes, glasses, etc. It had pass-through doors opening into each room for more convenience.

EATIN' GOOD IN OUR NEIGHBORHOOD

In the dining room we had a round, dark, solid-oak table with a large center pedestal. It was sturdy and big enough with its two wide extra leaves inserted to set places for Dad, Mama and seven kids for meals. These additional leaves were left in place all of the time. We didn't know about centerpieces, but Mama sometimes put a vase of freshly cut flowers from her garden in the middle of the table.

We had smooth-topped washable "oilcloth" table cloths, some flannel-backed, some plain and some floral patterned, even plaid, for everyday use, and beautifully hand-embroidered or crocheted table linens for Sunday or company use. Nothing was color-matched.

That big table took a beating. It was used not only for family dining three times a day but also for studying, games, ironing, etc. I didn't know until recently what happened to it after Dad died. Weldon says that Mama didn't use it at the little house when she moved, and not long after that he saw it in a ditch in the field close to the nearest sinkhole. It would have been an antique, scratched and dented a little, but I believe she didn't know of such things. It had served its purpose well over the years. Most of the chairs we used there were matched and they took a beating, too; there was also the ever-present high chair for many years.

Mealtime was a big deal; all of us ate every meal together at that big table in the dining room. There was room only for a small utilitarian table in the kitchen. I helped Mama cook the meals, Barb and Fran helped with the milking and also set the table and chairs. They were drawn into the cooking as they grew older. The boys helped with outside chores. Mama was adamant that we wash our hands before sitting down to eat. We ate what we put on our plates; none of us was a picky eater, but Russ' different foods couldn't touch on his plate. We were to try a very small helping of whatever Mama served. It was o.k. not to like it, but it was not o.k. not to taste it, and not o.k. to waste it.

It got to be pretty noisy many times. When everyone had finished eating, we could get up from the table. There were no TV sets, no computers, etc. available then as they are now. After supper and when all our chores and homework were done, we went outside in the fresh air to play until bedtime. In the cold of wintertime we played table games such as dominoes, jacks, puzzles, etc. or played on the floor with our toys. Sometimes there was good-natured kidding and sometimes there were loud disagreements, as you might expect in any group of kids of any age.

During my early years, we had an icebox, certainly not a very large one. It used big blocks of ice which were delivered by an "iceman" in the back of a big truck; a heavy canvas tarp covered the ice. In a few years we had a refrigerator fueled by a kerosene tank underneath. There was no room for bottled drinks, treats, etc. in it and, needless to say, there was no freezer for ice cream, etc.

Mama told us how, when she herself was a child, her father and neighbors--for storage purposes in the wintertime--built icehouses in their yards close to their houses. They used thick bales of straw for the sides and roofs and lined them with big ice blocks they cut out of the pond or nearby streams and covered them with tarps. These structures lasted long after the frigid winters and were in addition to the cellars on most farms.

Mama was a great cook and a good cooking teacher, too, tho' she did very little measuring, much of it done in the palm of her hand, which measurement would have been quite different in my small hand. She spent little time shopping for food in the nearby stores, except for things like rice, dried navy or pinto beans, macaroni, condiments such as coffee, sugar, salt, pepper, spices, syrups, etc. and some other things in the wintertime. She made her own dumplings and noodles from scratch.

She taught me at a young age to make baking powder biscuits from scratch for our meals, MADE AT LEAST TWICE EVERY DAY AND MOSTLY BY ME FOR MANY YEARS. Now, I buy biscuits already made--enough is enough! She also taught me to make cornbread, cakes and icing/frosting, pie crusts and fillings from scratch. Barb and Fran learned these things and others later. I loved crumbling any leftover cornbread into a glass of milk the next morning to be eaten with a spoon and I still enjoy it.

When we learned of real toast to be made from loaves of white (called "light") bread from the store, Mama bought a small toaster to be set on a gas stove burner. It had fold-down sides for two slices of bread; it darkened one side then the other side of the bread slice when it was turned by hand. It took a long time of constant watching and turning and several loaves of bread to make enough toast for everyone in our family to have a slice or two, or even longer if some had been burned, but we thought it was a wonderful treat.

When Mama had any extra time at all to do it, she made raised white yeast rolls for dinner. While they were "rising", she sent us kids outside to play so there would be no loud noises, no running or jumping, etc. that would cause the rolls to "fall". For a beautiful glaze, she whipped up several egg whites to spread on top of them just before baking. They were out-of-this-world delicious! Weldon sometimes took them to school to make a good trade, possibly for oranges, bananas, etc. when they might be available.

One day I ate most of the scrambled eggs I was making for our family breakfast, so Mama made me eat all those that were left. I had a similar experience with corn on the cob. Was I supposed to be perfect? We went through a lot of oatmeal, too, and cream of wheat.

Many, many times we had hot cornmeal mush for supper with cream and sugar. Leftovers, if any, were put into a deep wide dish overnight to cool and set; it was then sliced, seasoned with salt and pepper, and fried for the next day's breakfast, with butter spread over, and sometimes maple syrup. Delicious! Mama planned for leftover mashed potatoes and, if any, they were made into fried potato pancakes for breakfast or for supper later. For a change in her menu, Mama also served fluffy hot white rice for supper.

When I was big enough, I helped her wring the necks of the chickens for supper. The necks on my chickens got very, very, very long before the heads came off in my small hand. The bodies flopped around crazily in the grass for several minutes without their heads and we had to run them down. When I was a little older, this bothered me somewhat, although at that time and place such things were not considered to be cruelty to animals. We held them by the legs and dunked their bodies into a bucket of scalding water, plucked the feathers off, and carefully singed off with a burning piece of paper or cloth the little fine hairs that were left. A naked chicken with no head, flopping around in the grass, is not a pretty sight!

Mama taught me where to cut between the joints of the legs and where to cut off the wings, how to cut for a wishbone (the younger kids always wanted the wish bone), split the breasts, trim the backs, etc. I'm surprised I still like chicken and that I don't have a built-in aversion to the smell of it.

Mama had plenty of home-raised beef, pork and chicken readily available. Much of our meat, such as pounded beef round steak, pork chops and cut-up chicken (all of which were breaded) was fried in black wrought-iron skillets in the lard that during butchering pork had been rendered in our big black kettle outside. Some of us kids liked the fried chicken gizzards and livers. Chicken was served with mashed potatoes and white gravy made with milk and the drippings, thickened with flour and stirred continuously to be smooth as silk. Baking hens, pork and beef roasts (we didn't have "steaks") were roasted or baked and served with either thickened brown or clear gravy.

Mama shredded (or minced) and canned cooked seasoned meat for hash, etc. to be stored in the cellar for winter meals. These chores sometimes took almost all day long once she got started. In later years, we also had a freezer locker in town for meat not stored at home. We did not freeze fruits and vegetables then.

Sometimes we had the rabbits the boys caught in their traps, or the fish they caught. I couldn't get used to eating cute little rabbits. One day (out of season) a lone wild goose flew over and Dad shot it for supper--we were never to tell anyone, nor about the winter we had fresh deer meat out of season--one had somehow been hurt, strayed onto our land and paid dearly for it. I DID help eat them, but later wondered if these were "sins".

We always had all the milk, cream and eggs we needed for meals plus what we sold or traded to any of the nearby stores for something we might need at the time. The big depression did not affect farmers as much as it did city-folk.

Between the house and the carbide well, fenced off with wire fencing and gated from the back yard, was the large garden plot, neatly planted each year and overseen by Mama. Early each spring, Dad turned the dirt over (plowed it) and made the rows for her with his Farmall tractor and attached harrow. Long-handled hoes, forks, rakes, hand plows, spades and shovels were in their arsenal of garden tools for individual jobs. Gardens were a lot of work in those days; they required lots of weeding by hand and tools. Dad put up a big ugly wooden-frame scarecrow dressed in his old clothes and hat, hoping to scare away the many highly interested crows and rabbits; Old Pood was of no help at all!

Mama planted a big variety of vegetables, but rutabagas, parsnips, okra, etc. were not included. She took great pride in what she did grow, tending, harvesting, cooking, canning and sharing, etc. She bought little packets of seeds for many of the vegetables she planted. We cut pieces from seed potatoes and planted them eyes-up in rows and waited for them to sprout. We meticulously dropped kernels of seed corn in the long straight rows Dad made for her and planted climbing green beans beside the corn.

There were long, straight rows of yams, carrots, peas, beets, cabbage, spinach, cucumbers, rhubarb, green onions, radishes, leaf lettuce, a tomato patch, and other things usually found in a farmer's garden. I learned how to fix them her way. I helped her shell pleas, cut corn off the cob and snap green beans, whatever we were having for our meals. I stood at the stove and stirred creamed corn, usually singing to pass the time away. Pinto, navy or lima beans were cooked on low heat for 3 to 4 hours, seasoned most of the time with pieces of ham or bacon in them for flavor.

The green salads we had were cabbage slaw with a creamy dressing and wilted lettuce with warm homemade vinegar, oil and bacon-bits dressing. Many times Mama made sliced cucumber and onion salad with a vinegar, oil and sugar dressing. The first time I saw a combination lettuce salad many years later, I had no idea of how to eat it--the pieces looked much too large to put into my mouth! I copied my dining companions as they cut it into smaller pieces-- and what was that creamy pink "dressing" all about on top of it? It was not really a big hit with me for a long time. Mama did make devilled eggs, egg salad, potato salad, ham salad and macaroni salad sometimes, too.

In addition to cooking and canning meat, Mama home-canned vegetables and fruits, jams and jellies, and stored them on the cellar shelves for good eating later in the wintertime. One of my favorites was her own version of tomato preserves.

Mama had the orchard fruit trees, the grape arbor and the tame blackberry patch nearby. In the summertime we put single layers of grapes and cut-up apples on wax paper on the tin roof of the chicken house to be sun-dried and washed for eating or cooking later, whatever was left from the happy, thieving birds' raids. We raised watermelon, "mush-melon", popcorn and even peanuts one year. Try keeping kids out of those places.

Some wild plants were beautiful and some of them were edible, which took a discerning, experienced eye like Mama's to determine which were not poisonous. She taught us which wild "greens" to pick--plants which were prepared the same way that spinach was--but greens had just a little different taste each time, depending upon the plant selection made, and were not really to my liking, although now I think Mama should have been commended for trying different things. I wouldn't remember what to pick now after all this passed time.

There were big, fat wild blackberries, wild strawberries, and wild gooseberries in the fencerows and forests (gooseberry cobbler is still one of my very favorite desserts and my sister Fran makes the best!) There were paw-paw trees; their mild fruit was not a favorite with any of us.

For a few years we had several wooden bee hives halfway down the hill on the east side of the orchard and there was more than enough clover for them to use. The bees were far enough away that they never bothered us at the house and yards and we seldom saw them. We watched from a distance behind the trees in the orchard when the grownups donned their heavy clothes and gloves and the big-brimmed hats with netting hanging down over their faces and necks.

They ventured forth to gather the honey the bees had placed in the waxy honeycomb cells they made in the little square wooden boxes Dad had put in their hives. The bees immediately became fighting mad and came out buzzing and swarming in busy circles around the intruders! On a few occasions, at least one of us would have a fresh bee sting someplace on us. Honey did not have to be preserved to stay fresh nor did the sorghum molasses Mama and Dad made from some of the sargo crop, most of which had been cut up into ensilage or put in shocks for animal feed later in the winter.

There were no frozen or boxed ready-made dinners and/ or dinner helpers. Neither were there ready mixes available for cakes, pancakes, pies, biscuits, cornbread, dressings, etc. Women had to make everything from scratch. Mama didn't have a shelf full of exotic spices or wines, either.

We didn't know about chili, tacos, enchiladas, etc., pizza had yet to be "invented", but we had wonderful homemade soups and stews. We had homemade egg noodles and dumplings. Mama bought white rice at the store and used it in many ways; she also bought elbow macaroni and cooked it with tomatoes--cheese was hard as a rock, we didn't like the taste, and it didn't cook well. We also didn't know about spaghetti and meat sauce. It was much, much later when we heard of cottage cheese and none of us was fond of that.

Mama's pies--these, too, were made from memory--were out-of-this world delicious, with their flaky crusts and full-bodied puddings, golden-browned meringue toppings, or with their fresh fruit fillings. Homemade whipped cream was available within a few minutes of the asking; it and meringue were made with a small hand-powered mixer. (One weekend I had some friends from college stay over. To everyone's delight, Mama had the dining room table covered with pies of all kinds--fruit pies and cream pies--when we arrived. What a wonderful surprise treat for us!)

She made the best burnt-sugar cake you can imagine, but used no recipe, much to the dismay of many women. She taught us to make various kinds of cookies. We never had a store-bought pie or cake; cookies bought were fig Newtons, sometimes ginger snaps or such.

We did not eat out in restaurants, cafes, diners, etc. when we were very young children growing up. We didn't even know they were available for dining. There certainly were no fast-food eateries around, although we heard there were hotdog street vendors in town. Our own kitchen and dining room and those of kin and neighbors were all we knew, except for the picnics our families had at different times at various parks, or perhaps the hot dogs sold by vendors at fairs. This was true through our grade school years.

I do not remember even one meal shared with my whole family in a dining establishment of any kind.

Annabelle says Mama was considered to be the best cook around. Everything was tasty and made from scratch from the recipes in Mama's head or maybe something she made up on the spur of the moment. If she lacked some kind of an ingredient, she had an instinctive idea of what to substitute for it. None of it was extra fancy, gourmet food. I believe some of her intuitive talent had been passed down from her Dutch mother.

I sat down to rest for a few minutes in the recliner. As I have grown older, my rest periods have grown longer and more frequent. I don't remember that Mama took some time out for a much-needed rest. If she sat down during the day, she had a lap full of one of the kids who just needed a sympathetic, warm loving hug or many times a crying kid that needed a bandage. She had potatoes to peel, or a mess of beans to string and snap for dinner. Sometimes it was an accidental kid-caused spill, or maybe a load of wash that was ready to be hung out on the line.

Her days were always full, and she had no place to retreat, even if she had wanted to do so.

She certainly didn't have time to sit down to read a novel, magazine, or newspaper. She was too busy to sit down to write letters, thank-you cards or party invitations. I don't remember that any Christmas cards, birthday or sympathy cards were ever sent out. There were no bills paid by mail. For people like us, there was very little correspondence by mail, although stamps would have been only 2 or 3 cents each then. Idly chatting on that big wall phone with relatives or friends and neighbors wasn't in her plan for the day either. We did keep in contact by our visiting in the homes of friends and relatives.

DAD'S SIDE

Dad, THE SECOND CHILD, WAS born March 23, 1892, at the family farm home in Christian County, Missouri. It was a one-story white house a mile or so down a country road south of the mailbox corner. He moved with his family into their larger new home nearby when it was built several years later, across the county line into Greene County a mile and a half away. I was told that I was born in the new house on November 27, 1925. Grandpa John and Grandma Malda Notie Elizabeth Howell Cinderella Lousanna Jane (Wills) Fulton had moved to "town" at the time. Dad and his brothers helped with farm chores. There were eight children.

When Grandma and Grandpa moved back to the farm shortly after my birth, our family moved into the "lower place" for a few years. I have a picture Mama took there of me as a baby, hanging at the end of a full-size sheet pinned on me like a diaper. It had been hung up on a clothesline with huge wooden clothes pins. I guess that was her baby sitter and it was certain that I wasn't going any place! The lower place is where Jake and Wade were born.

One day when Jake, toddler Wade and I were playing in the front yard there we saw a big strange dog trotting down the road toward us, head and tail down. Jake took a firm hold of Wade's hand and we ran into the house. I think now how instinctively brave and thoughtful he was at such a young age.

We kids never knew Dad's brother, Uncle Glen. He died at age twenty-four in late 1918 in France in World War I shortly after he was called to duty, and was later returned home and buried in the National Cemetery in Springfield.

I barely remember Dad's youngest brother, Uncle Johnny, who was a young, funny boy, always laughing and cutting up when we saw him. Yelling and laughing out loud, he drove the wagon and horses up and down those hilly, rough, rocky roads so fast the wooden wagon with its steel wheels bounced around and drove Grandpa wild. I was almost six years old when he was accidentally killed at age twenty-two while he was hunting with Uncle Glen's automatic rifle, just a week before his mother's birthday. I do remember that he was fun when he played with us, a lot.

I don't remember much about Grandma Fulton either, except that she was tall and slim and she wore her dark gray hair pulled back into a bun, as did so many women then. I've been told that she and Grandpa John moved to Springfield after Uncle Johnny's funeral and we moved back from the lower place into the big farmhouse. She died shortly after that (it was said she died of heartbreak) and Grandpa moved back with us on the farm.

Mama took constant care of Grandpa for awhile in a bed set up in the living room when he was very ill with "consumption". He put his hand on my head and held my ear against the mound of his big fat belly. I was fascinated by the loud rolling, gurgling noises but Mama told me not to bother him too much. He had been such a loving, jolly man, always laughing a lot and teasing us kids. His brother, Uncle Ab, who lived in town, resembled him a lot and died of the same thing. I wonder what name it goes by now. I missed Grandpa John so much after he was gone.

Two of my father's sisters, Aunt Beulah and Aunt Leta, and their families lived nearby; the others lived out-of-state, but we saw them in the summertime most of the years. When they visited us--always in the heat of summer--some of them got to stay in our bedrooms and all we kids gleefully made do with old quilts and blankets spread out on the lawn. Once in a while I did get to admire their clothes hanging in our small closets when they visited relatives elsewhere; I even sneaked a try-on when I could, whirling and twirling, and thought they would never know.

We had lots of company, mostly family--aunts, uncles, cousins; we were related in some way to so many of the people who lived anywhere around us. The back screened-in porch was a favorite place for our elders to gather; in the wintertime the living room was used. They shut the door between the living room and the dining room where we kids and our cousins played. They had to shut out what they could of the noise we made, but checked on us or called us down occasionally by rapping on the glass window in the top half of the door between the rooms.

These were mostly visits after all chores were finished, after supper or after Sunday dinner; no food was served. When supper was over, eating was over. We knew nothing of "chips and dips and veggies" or such; sometimes we had popcorn or home-made candy, partly for the pure fun of making and sharing it. If anyone were thirsty, there was plenty of good, cold drinking water, or sometimes the adults drank iced tea or coffee. There was no sitting around drinking beer, hard liquor, or even "soft" drinks.

Many, many times in the evenings we children sat quietly, depending on the time of year, in the corners and against the walls of the back porch or the living room. We loved to hear the stories our aunts and uncles told about their own childhoods and about other people--relatives and neighbors. There was so much laughter and it got to be pretty loud wherever they were. Now, I wish I could remember their stories about those days and the "olden" days before. They had many arguments about politics and religion, too. We also visited in their homes nearby. I know they exist, but I can't imagine being in truly dysfunctional families, fighting, not speaking for years, if ever, etc.

Before W.W. II people married and lived within the nearby neighborhoods. The war, with all its inventions and opportunities, opened up to young people an opportunity and means to travel to far away places to live and work, so that attendance at big family get-togethers just dropped off and family connections were never the same again.

I had great cousins, both male and female. Annabelle was a favorite of mine from the time I was very young. She was fun and always there for me, living just down the road a piece--and she still is.

I saw Bonabeth, Aunt Leta and Uncle Roy Mallonee's daughter, a lot. When they lived in Sparta, Missouri, we were very young kids. I wanted and tried to spend the night there on many occasions, but at times Uncle Roy, bless his kind heart, had to bring me home in the middle of the night. I don't to this day know why I did that--I wasn't a spoiled kid. I think now that he shouldn't have given in to me; I really feel badly about that now that I'm a grownup.

For two years we went to the same high school after Uncle Roy came back from working for a while on the Alaskan Highway Project, bought a new car, and moved from Sparta to a farm near us. Bonabeth and I were in the same classes and had the same friends; we liked to do the same things and we spent lots of time together. A lot of that time we were just mooning over boys, and we double dated; she liked to plan her future with every cute boy she met, trying on his last name; they all fit for a little while--until the next one came along. Now--great husband, great kids.

She was fun and very pretty, looked like her dad. She was also a little bossy, for being only a few months older than I. At one of the family picnics I heard a couple of our aunts discussing how pretty Bonabeth was and how sad it was that I was so plain. I remember that once in a while and think it may have had something to do with how unsure of myself and how self-conscious I was growing up later and am even now sometimes. At that time, though, I didn't have time to worry about it; it wasn't important then.

Bonabeth's brother, Allen, was a cutie, too, and had a wonderful sense of humor--funny, funny, always ready to take a dare or challenge. He was the same age as Jake and they and Wade spent a lot of time together, sometimes with their other friends, mostly doing mischievous things. He died many years ago after marrying and having a family.

They had another brother, James, years later (a change-of-life baby) but I didn't get to know him at all; I always heard that he was wilder than a March hare. Many years later during a drought year, Russ and my husband John helped him haul water from a nearby river in a big, round steel tank at the back of a truck bed. The filled tank was heavy, and the water sloshed back and forth so hard that it made the front tires of the truck bounce on and off the ground all the way home, spilling much of the water. There are many funny tales told about James.

Kathleen, the daughter of Aunt Lena and Uncle Harrison Fulton (Grandpa John's brother), was a few years older than I and taught us how to play some card games. They lived on a farm just down the road west of Aunt Ida, next to the fenced and gated Fulton Cemetery. Kathleen came over some Sundays and helped us make taffy--what fun that was to stretch it out as far as we could between us and run to fold it back upon itself, then repeat the process until it was ready! She married and lives on an Indian

Reservation with her husband and family, and is another favorite I haven't seen since graduation, regrettably.

In one of my old black-and-white individual grade school picture albums Kathleen's face is turned to the side because she had a big red, oozy boil on one side of her nose. That picture turned out to be a big mistake because the bandage shows below her nose and makes it look as if she had a terribly messy, runny cold. BUT she's in the album!

Uncle Harrison's oldest daughter, Dorothy, is Annabelle's age and was a schoolteacher in the area later. Her husband Charles was a brother of Bert, Annabelle's husband. One of the sons, Gene, and his wife Muriel lived in Springfield. I don't remember Linuel, the other brother, much at all.

One of our distant cousins built a candy room onto their home and made hard candy for sale commercially. We kids especially loved the striped ribbon candy which had been stretched and folded back onto itself, then stretched and folded again and again, leaving colorful 1" wide loops, made in holiday colors and patterns every year at Christmas time. They also made different types of chocolates and other candies.

When I bring up cousins, no way can I leave out Nita, Aunt Maisie (Pad) and Uncle Carl Wheeler's daughter, two-plus years older than I. She was the one from Texas with the long drawn-out drawl and a cute chuckle. When they came to visit family in the summertime, she would part my hair in the middle and make a "cowpile" on top of each side; I didn't think it looked too pretty, but Nita did it so it was o.k. and what did I know anyway? She also took it upon herself to teach me how to kiss--on the back of my hand--at a very young age. Later, I was grateful for that, but at the time I wondered why in the world I needed to know.

She was the ringleader when it came to organizing neighborhood hay rides, and the buggy and horseback rides for just the two of us. That shiny old black buggy, with black double front and back leather seats, was in excellent condition and got a lot of use by all of us and our friends; we loved riding in it with Old Bessie harnessed up in front to pull it.

When I was about twelve, Nita and I saddled up and rode our horses all the way to Ozark one day, stopping for that NUDE swim Nita took in the river, yelling and laughing, jumping and splashing, and trying to coax me into coming in. No way! I was extremely nervous as I sat on the river bank holding her clothes, my head busy turning in every direction to look for anyone who might be coming that way. What would I have done if someone had come along?

Nita had us dropping by later at some stranger's home in Ozark; she went up to his door and "borrowed" twelve cents from him for pop with some wild story about paying him back one day soon. Sadly, she lost her husband a few years ago, but has a very supportive family around her. Nita now has her own place in Florida with many horses of her own. She has visited with us a couple of times for the family 4th. Her twin brother Carl, called "Bud", was quieter and mostly laughed at the antics of everyone else. Nita was another "older sister" I never had. No, the twelve cents was never repaid to that nice man, who probably didn't expect to see it again; with interest it must be a sizeable debt now, payable to his heirs.

Nita and I were very close with Reba, Uncle Baxter (Grandma Fulton's brother) and Aunt Mary Wills' fun daughter who was a couple of years older than Nita, and she rode her horse through those dusty country roads with us many times.

She has a lovely, go-getter sister, Kathryn, who is Annabelle's age. Because I moved away after graduation, I did not get to know her and their younger sister, Harriet, better, along with their respective families. From time to time I can see how much Kathryn and my sister Fran resemble each other in their facial expressions.

Reba helped me get my first job after high school graduation. It was in a war-time men's pants factory in Springfield; another girl and I, one on each side, ran with the khaki-colored cotton fabric from one end of the long table to the other. The fabric billowed high into the air and other workers caught it and laid it straight in many layers to be cut according to pattern by big jigsaws hanging on a metal runner from the ceiling.

One day after a full day's work there, I was casually walking home to my apartment and met a man on the sidewalk who opened his long coat and showed me everything he had; he was stark naked. He said nothing; neither did I, but I was way much faster leaving the scene than he. Reba laughed when I told her, but advised me to be careful, and to take a different route home after that. This was a new and surprising experience for me, but I wasn't scared.

There were two cousins from Wisconsin, Aunt Ana and Uncle Clarence Egdahl's kids Gwenny and Sonny, about the same ages as the others. The southerners and hillbillies understood very little of what they said--they talked a lot, at least twice as fast as any of us, and in a funny dialect! We kinda just gawked at 'em and tried to understand what they were saying, but they were fun as they joined in all our games. I wonder what they reported to their hometown friends.

Gwenny was hit in one eye by a small piece of carbide that bounced up as we watched the carbide being poured into the carbide well one summer day. That was the saddest of the visits then; there were no other serious accidents in all those years of family visits. I heard later that she was blinded in that eye, but I don't know for sure. I tried unsuccessfully for several years to contact Gwenny or Sonny or their kids, if any. As with so many of our relatives, I wish now we had kept in contact with them. I heard from Bonabeth that they both passed away several years ago.

Aunt Beulah (Dad's oldest sister) and Uncle Paul Cowan had three children, a little older than the other cousins. They lived on a farm north of us across that graveled Highway 60; it was another good place to visit, yet another barn and yard to play in; more good fun and food at family picnics. Aunt Beulah died March 6, 1974.

Their son Jerry was the oldest of the "first cousins"--smart, handsome and soooo nice, always coming to visit or to help with anything he could. He was busy with his own carpentry business in Springfield when he grew up and had a family, but he still took time to visit us often. He was good, strong, willing help when needed and he and his family lived near his old home.

Orene was the next of their children, dark and pretty, so witty and quick with her thoughts, so funny, always joking and laughing. She and Jerry looked like their dad. She was the smartest of us all, I've heard. She later moved away and worked for some department in the state government.

Glen, the youngest of their children, was about three years older than I and was named after Dad's brother. He was a little heavy, I remember, and was nicknamed "Hoogie"; he was fun to be around, although he was the one who told me there was no Santa; I think I was about 12.

Aunt Thora, called "Kiddo", was the youngest of Dad's sisters, born in 1916, nine years after Johnny was born. She was best buddies with her cousin Annabelle Scott. I have heard they, mostly Kiddo, were pretty wild for that day and time. Kiddo's favorite expression was "Dad burn it!" and she had a hearty laugh. Annabelle says she never knew what Kiddo would come up with next. She had a big old terrapin pet she called Old Mo who got lost somehow but made Kiddo happy by coming back home later. He, being a turtle, probably hadn't traveled far from home.

Kiddo met and married Henry Cordes in Arizona where she was living at that time with her sister, Aunt Pad, and her family. Henry was tall, straight and darkly handsome; Kiddo was short and pretty. His father and mother were native German immigrants who met in New York and moved to Arizona in 1883.

One summer, many years ago, she brought Henry and their very young girls, Patsy and Anita, back to Missouri to her old home to meet her family. She passed away September 27, 1975. On a wall in their old house in Cordes, Arizona, Henry kept a black-and-white 8x10 wedding picture of them taken so many years ago.

They worked hard in that barren desert land on their large range where horses and cattle roamed. We had heard a story of how she was caught in the desert in a flash flood one day and saved herself by grabbing and hanging onto a scrubby cactus shrub and she had some bloody scratches to prove it. From all accounts, she was a scrappy, fun-loving person and a hard worker.

Nita, John and I visited Henry and the girls a few years ago and were amazed at how much they still resemble their mother. Henry took us to a field fenced in with barbed wire; we three climbed through the fence and walked through the fields where horses and cattle roamed to a canyon and mesa where Nita could visit the old Richinbar gold and silver mine which had been opened in 1896, four miles east of Bumble Bee, where her Dad (who had been a well-to-do geologist in Houston), had worked, and the area where her family had lived. She and her twin brother

Carl, Jr, (Bud) were very young in 1936, and attended school in Phoenix.

When the mine closed in 1937, everyone left but their family; electricity was turned off, and they had to haul water and used a Coleman stove for cooking. They lived there for two more years, a very primitive life, hunting game for food. She has great tales to tell about that part of her life.

Nita has been instrumental in helping to get a wonderfully interesting article published about this area and subject through Friends of the Agua Fria National Monument; information is available @ 623-580-5500 or at www.bim.gov/az. For information on the interviews with Nita and Bud, you may contact Sandy Gauthier @602-569-1526, or contact Nita Underwood herself @850-592-3333.

Uncle Henry was in his upper nineties when he died; his face wore the colors of the painted desert around him; he became much shorter in recent years, stooped over from age and hard work. He was loving and generous, his mind still sharp as a tack. He married--some years after Aunt Kiddo's death--Sylvia (deceased now), an old friend and widowed neighbor, and was getting around great for a long time.

Long ago, he worked for the Pony Express at the Cordes Stage Stop, which had been established by his father; it also became a post office for a while, a supply depot and a bank for the miners until the main highway to Flagstaff passed it by about three miles away to the east. That junction on

Interstate Highway 17 is named Cordes Junction. When we visited him last in Cordes, he still lived in their house (the old Pony Express depot) that is over one hundred thirty years old.

He and daughter Anita cooked a big roast and all the fixin's, including dessert, for his brother Carl, me, my husband John, Nita, Patsy and Anita, their menfolk, and their kids and grandkids. We were joined later by two of his long-time friends--one a preacher--who sang and played guitars and other instruments for us.

I loved to hear the tales he told and the tales they told about him. His life and occupation were written up in articles in at least three magazines a few years back. In fact, I loved him very much for what he was and for the different world he presented to us. I am so sorry that Aunt Kiddo didn't live many years longer to enjoy him and her growing family.

Anita and her husband, Bill Willis, visited us in Arizona after a recent trip to Cordes. They confirmed that the old house is still standing. There are remnants of the old boarding houses out back, in bad shape but still holding some valuable antiques, and these buildings will be torn down when the antiques are removed.

Across the road from Henry's old house, the once-busy old country store/filling station/depot with its old red gasoline pump is still there and is being converted into an antique shop by one of the granddaughters. Many things are being found that Anita and Patsy can't part with, she said, things that bring back memories of their folks and their earlier years and are so dear to them.

Our two "Anita" cousins came back recently to Missouri to spend the 4th of July with my sisters and brothers and their families; it was a wonderful time of reminiscing and visiting the graveyard of so many kin. They got to see Bonabeth and her family. They visited with Annabelle and enjoyed her talking and telling tales about their Mom. We took them to Branson to enjoy a wonderful show.

Dad's large Fulton/Wills family married into other large families named Campbell, Cowan, Miller, etc. and we can rarely go someplace where we don't find relatives.

MAMA'S FOLKS

MAMA WAS BORN ON A farm in Greene County, Missouri, on July 17, 1896, the second daughter; she had three sisters and one brother. Because her parents came from the "old country", she didn't have a large, close, extended family and friends around her as Dad did, and she told me that she and her siblings spoke German and very little English up until the time they entered grade school. I wish I had learned some German from her and that she had written down their relatives' names and where they might be found.

Mama's mother, Grandma Frances Anna Beriend (Fran is named after her), was a short, round little woman I barely remember. Her long fine gray hair was pulled back into a bun with a beautiful decorative comb at the back of her head, and Grandmas did not wear makeup in those days. She had come to America on a boat from Austria. She was very loving and--as most women seemed to do back then-- was always cooking something and offering us good things to eat. I'm sure that much of Mama's culinary expertise was learned from her.

Mama's father, Jacob Braun (Jake is named after him and Grandpa John), came from Switzerland. The few pictures I have of him show a big man with a big moustache, always dressed up.

I have heard that he and Grandma were both young when they met; I don't really know how or where, but I heard they met on that boat. He passed away before we kids were born and we didn't have Grandma Frances nearly long enough either. When did they marry; what were the circumstances that brought them into the southwest corner of Missouri of all places? Why didn't I ask someone long ago who could tell me?

Mama's youngest sister, Aunt Lydia--never married and long since gone from us now--visited their families overseas many years ago but failed to write anything down. She did bring home a few pictures of the homes and family. At that time I was too young and self-absorbed to care. I could have learned so much from her.

Our cousin Hazel is the daughter of Mama's oldest sister, Aunt Clara, and Uncle Dave Logan. She is near Annabelle's age. She recently gave me copies that Aunt Lydia had given her of a picture of Grandpa Jacob's home in Switzerland, and one of Grandma Frances' home in Austria; both pictures are somewhat blurry. Both looked to be very large 2-story homes with many windows. She also gave me a studio picture of Grandma and her brothers. They all resembled each other, mainly through the nose and eyes. In spite of that, none of us, including Mama, seem to resemble them at all.

Hazel gave me a few pictures taken at the farm home where Mama and her family grew up; it was a white two-story home that was located a few miles north of our home. Her father is shown standing beside a beautiful old car in front of their home. There are two wagons holding Grandma and the girls, Aunt Clara, Aunt Sophie, Aunt Lydia and Mama; their brother, Uncle Carl, is in the background. There is also a later picture of Mama and her brother and sisters sitting on the porch of their home when they were much older; very little of the home is shown.

I would like to see pictures of Mama when she was a baby. In the one old formal family studio picture Hazel gave me, Mama is a child about six years old with a halo of blond curls; Aunt Lydia, the youngest child of the family, is not in it. All three sisters in the picture are dressed in long, dark, heavy, yoked dresses, with wrist length sleeves and high necklines, nothing of their bodies showing but faces and hands. Grandpa Jacob and Uncle Carl are wearing suits and ties. Again, no one is smiling. There are no pictures of them playing in the yard or sitting around posing, and so far I have seen no school pictures.

I like the snapshot we have of Mama when she was still a teenager, standing in their yard, wearing a fancy dress with her hair piled up on top of her head in the style of the times, and the studio picture of her and another young woman--a sister? a friend?--wearing dark dresses and small black helmet-like hats called cloches covering their hair and much of their faces. In most of the pictures I've seen, Mama is wearing different hats, most of them big-brimmed, shading her face. There are no really clear pictures of any of the shoes or boots they may have been wearing. It seems to be certain, however, that ladies of that era loved to wear hats of all sizes and shapes, but I have seen no pictures of purses they may have carried.

One snapshot shows Mama when she was probably in her early twenties, hair pulled up on top of her head, when she had an 18" waistline; she didn't know then that many years later she would have seven children and be much heavier! Some people think Fran and I resemble her in different ways as she looked then.

I wish that she had told me more about her family and what she liked to do as a young child, what games they played, what toys they had, what their clothes were like, their school years--what school?--and what she was like as a young woman. Did she have close girl friends and keep them for many years? Did she have many beaus? It never occurred to me to ask her questions like these when I was growing up; I took her for granted just as she appeared to me. I was like most kids, not knowing or caring at that age; now, as an adult, I care very much.

Mama said that she and her sisters, dressed in high-topped shoes, long skirts, long sleeves and bonnets, along with Uncle Carl, picked strawberries and other crops to be sold by her and/or her father to the various grocers in town. They did not have the large herds of cattle, hogs, sheep, big crops, etc. as Dad's family did, although there was a barn and there were other small buildings. It has been my understanding that Grandpa Braun worked in town somewhere.

The living room and (later) Aunt Sophie's bedroom on the first floor of their home were separated from the kitchen-dining area by a covered porch open from the front of the house through to the back yard, and there was a narrow porch with a few chairs facing out in front of the kitchen. There were two bedrooms upstairs. All of the rooms were under the same roof, though, and they all had linoleum floors and wallpaper on the plastered walls. There were no indoor bathrooms there, either.

There was the usual mounded, grass-topped dirt storm cellar in the yard, close to the house, half out and half dug into the ground, where Grandmother Frances stored her canned fruits, vegetables, etc. and our Grandfather Jacob stored the wine he made. Mama told us that many of his bottles exploded. Most homesteads around us had these storm cellars in some form or another, as there were no basements.

In the yard off to one side was a rough straw and sawdust structure used as an ice house in the wintertime; it lasted long after the frigid ice melted. Ice was sawed out of the pond and carried there by horse and wagon.

In the kitchen there was a huge black iron stove which burned small logs (banked at night) and there was always water steaming away in a big black tea kettle sitting there on a burner, ready to make coffee at a moment's notice. The stove had a big baking oven below the burners and there was a line of warming ovens across the back above the regular burners. As in our home, there was the big round oak table with its two extra leafs and many straight ladder-back chairs.

The wonderful smell of fresh baked loaves of homemade "light" bread or rolls and sometimes cinnamon rolls greeted us when we visited there. Our unmarried Aunt Sophia lived there with Mama's brother, Uncle Carl, after their parents were gone, then lived there by herself when he left, and we visited her often. She, too, wore her long black hair pulled back into a bun. She giggled a lot and, like the others, was very sweet. She kept mothballs in her closet, so I didn't even want to try on her clothes. We loved the few pictures she showed us of Mama's family; I wish I had them now.

Unlike Dad's family, Mama's sisters and brother were fairly short. Uncle Carl was a wiry man with dark brown hair, and was very witty. In addition to his regular farming, Uncle Carl always grew a large patch of the best watermelons around. He loaded them onto a large flatbed wagon piled with hay to protect them, pulled by a team of horses, and hauled them around the rough gravel roads to us and sold them to other neighbors that might want them. My brother Russell was named Carl after him. Russ grew up to be a watermelon grower, too, sharing them with us.

Uncle Carl had been "shell-shocked" in World War I and later lived in a Veterans' Hospital in Arkansas, where John and I visited him. I don't remember his wife at all. Our cousin Manuel was his son and we didn't see much of him or his family after we all grew up, though we had played so often with him as kids. He passed away many years ago.

Aunt Clara, Mama's oldest sister, and Uncle Dave Logan and family lived a few miles away from the old home; they had two children, Hazel and Benn, a few years older than I. Hazel looked a lot like her mother then and still does, very pretty, very feminine, soft-spoken. They wore soft curls- -no buns pulled back--around their faces and wore pretty, feminine clothes. Benn, a tall nice-looking redhead, was very intelligent and was a collector of old bathtubs, sinks, farm machinery and other antiques in later years. We only recently lost him; he was still a handsome, sweet man.

Aunt Lydia, the youngest sister, had beautiful auburn red hair and wore it shorter than the others, curled slightly; she was always smiling. She never married and lived in Washington, D.C.; she worked for the government for many years, and we didn't see her often enough. Sometimes she sent us big boxes of children's beautiful dresses, coats, shoes and toys that were outgrown by her boss' family but very much appreciated by Mama. It has always been thought that Russ got his red hair from this side of the family and passed it on to his kids, and then to their kids. As far as I know, one aunt in Dad's family was redheaded.

Many of my aunts had names that ended on an "up" sound; they were Leta, Beulah, Clara, Ana, Sophia, Thora, Ida, Lydia, Lena, and others such as Emma, our Mama. Barb and I weren't named after any of them but Fran has the names of Mama's mother Frances and Dad's Aunt Minnie. Down through the years, though, the names of long-gone relatives have been given to many boy grandchildren and even passed down from there, especially in Dad's family.

Having all this family gave us kids such a feeling of belonging and we still have it with each other today.

SOME FOLKS NOT KIN

FRIENDLY TRAVELING SALESMEN WOULD OFTEN drive through our part of the country; we were never afraid of these strangers. Mama bought from many of them, the regulars, but decided not to one day and instructed us to tell the Raleigh man she wasn't there. Weldon told the salesman that she was in the closet and she said to tell him she wasn't home. The Raleigh man laughed and left.

From time to time during the late spring, summer and fall months, gypsies would travel through our part of the country and stay someplace for a few days. They camped out under some trees down the road from our house, fishing for perch and catfish in our dirty old pond nearby, before they moved on in their covered wagons with clothes, clanging pots and pans hanging on the sides as they moved on to stay at another farm nearby.

Mama and Dad gave them firewood, water and milk, a couple of chickens, bacon and some other meat to cook in their kettles on their big bonfires, and fruit and vegetables from the garden.

They looked and dressed so differently in those bright, colorful clothes that we couldn't help but stare as we peeked from behind the orchard trees. The women wore long, gathered wild-print skirts with lots of ruffles and blouses with large puffy sleeves. The gypsies sang songs we didn't understand, played musical instruments and danced in the dust by firelight, accompanied by loud laughter wafting into the evening skies across the whole area. This was another time that Mama herded us close to the house until the "stranger danger" passed. Now, of course, I realize they weren't interested in us at all.

During the 30s, prohibition was the big thing--the days of bootlegging, Pretty Boy Floyd, Baby Face Nelson, John Dillinger in Chicago, Bonnie and Clyde robbing banks in small towns in Missouri, and many others.

To us the word "foreigner" was only a word in a book. We thought everyone was like us. We took the blue sky, white clouds, sun, the moon and stars for granted and never thought of "outer space" except perhaps in a geography or science lesson, and certainly could not have imagined going there. We had not heard of an alien…huh?

THE GROUNDS

Nᴏʀᴛʜ ᴏꜰ ᴏᴜʀ ʜᴏᴜꜱᴇ ʙᴇʜɪɴᴅ a wire fence was a big wooden barn, facing south, painted "barn" red, with its huge hinged front double-doors, which were seldom shut. There was a loft all across the top of the barn which was usually full of loose, new, fresh-smelling hay as well as the baled. Much of our time was spent in the barn; many nights in nice weather or during a softly falling rain we kids took old blankets up to the loft to make soft beds and slept on the hay. Knowing that playing in the hay would cause constant itching and scratching later did not take away the fun of it.

The barn was home to many barn owls and a few bats, but I don't recall that we were ever afraid of them. We saw an occasional mouse but mice fought a continuing losing battle with the several cats that also lived in the barn. We were familiar with all the other animals (and their noises) that might be around the barn, too.

We kids loved playing and rough-housing in that barn. I don't think our parents knew about some of the potentially dangerous things we were doing there. The big hay fork suspended by a heavy chain and ropes from a large beam at the top of the inside roof was used for unloading both the baled hay and the loose hay from the wagons delivering it from the fields. We learned to work the ropes to swing on it way out from the loft through the open double doors to the ground; dismount was easy and not dangerous.

We had left-handed corncob fights there regularly; one of those hard, scratchy cobs left a large red imprint on Jake's forehead that lasted several days and we had an occasional bruise on us someplace. We and our friends and cousins played "hide and seek" in the barn. One of the kids wouldn't be "it"; he went to the house and didn't come back until someone else gave in and volunteered to be "it" in his place. Sometimes we just rolled or scuffled in the soft hay. Certainly a visit with the hose at the house was called for after all this.

Tall, round, plain gray concrete silos that looked like upright tubes stood, one on the east and one on the west sides of the barn, open at the top. In late summer, corn silage for feeding cattle was blown into the tops of each silo through tall pipes from a machine on the ground cutting the corn stalks into small pieces. Each silo had a small square, open window way up high, used to check periodically on the amount and condition of the silage. A narrow staircase inside the barn led to staggered entries into the silos.

When I was in my early teens, the old red barn burned down; it was late one evening in the fall when, luckily, there was no wind, but there was no way to save it. It was a huge, fast-burning fire, crackling and flaring up into the darkening sky, with choking black smoke, red, yellow and orange flame fingers and bright white sparks flying high into the air. It wasn't long before many concerned neighbors gathered to watch and help in any way they could, bringing water from the nearby well-house, relating tales of other barn fires they had seen. Internal combustion was the cause, the men said--the big hay crop was too green to have been "put up" when it was. It was, of course, a losing battle.

The men made sure that all the animals were outside of the barn; if any weren't, the men were nice enough not to tell us kids. Soon everybody was running around, yelling and scratching because little black fleas were fleeing the fire and looking for new homes.

Meanwhile, I ran to the house, up to my bedroom; I carried/slid my mattress and bedding down the stairs and out into the yard to keep it safe in case the house burned. It took two men to return it upstairs to my room. Russ followed me with a small stuffed toy. Weldon carried his toys out into the yard. Jake and Wade were in the middle of helping the men checking the fire and moving things away from the barn. Dad was gone from home on a cattle-buying trip and could hardly believe what had happened while he was away.

Many neighbor men came later to help with the new "barn raising" between the still-standing silos which had been darkened by the smoke but left unharmed. Hammers and other tools fell from their hands occasionally and anyone on the ground had to be wary. The men always enjoyed these shared adventures. Their womenfolk brought food and made a party of the whole thing.

It would never be quite the same to us kids; we had loved the old red barn like family and would remember for many years all the fun we had had there. We adapted to the new barn very quickly, however.

Each summer there were wild, thorny, large-leafed, sturdy, evil-smelling dark green weeds with big beautiful white trumpet-shaped flowers scattered throughout the barnyard area; even the livestock wouldn't eat them. There was a muddy, fenced-in plot where the swine "lived", oinking, grunting and snorting constantly. Cattle, dairy cows and their calves, sheep, goats, horses, etc. roamed the fenced fields nearby.

Some of the fences that enclosed fields where cattle, horses and other large animals were kept were made of several rows of barbed wire and after a few bad experiences with those, we became very careful about climbing through or over them. Some fences had a single row of barbed wire at the top of other fencing for smaller animals. We didn't know then of stiles, although they may have been used on other farms.

Always looking for something to do, we kids tried to walk in the wheat piled high in the small grain house nearby; none of us knew just how dangerous that fun was. I shudder now to think that we could have been pulled down by gravity and suffocated in all that slick grain as we sank deeper and deeper with each step or movement. Mama couldn't watch every move we made and might have fainted away if she had known it all.

The long (it seemed long to us back then) dirt/gravel drive ended at the barn gate. Just short of that on the east was the rock well-house building which faced west; it had a deep fresh-water well, a work bench, and some storage space for dairy things, farm machinery and tools. Water from that well was also piped underground to the main house into a big reservoir in the attic over the kitchen area and down into the kitchen sink--unheated. This was our second source of water at the house. For a while we had a third source of water--there had been a covered cistern in the yard outside the kitchen, but it was closed not long after we moved back the last time.

For a few years when Dad was alive, to shorten the need for trips to town, we had our own big red gasoline pump near the well-house. Dad was neat with the machinery; it was not stored close to the house or in the yard, but kept behind fences or the barn. Maybe Mama had something to do with that.

Just south of the well-house was the long, narrow one-story chicken house. Built waist-high around the room onto the walls, just over the top of a long cabinet, was a row of wooden nest boxes lined with straw, changed often, from which to gather the eggs laid there daily. Big black snakes curled up sometimes in the nests where I gathered eggs. I had been told they were harmless, but ... Sometimes we could see the shape of an unbroken egg inside the snake's body.

The brooder house was close by. In the springtime when Mama brought home large numbers of little, white baby Leghorn chicks from the hatchery in town, I sat on the floor in the middle of them, watching and listening, fascinated by their beauty, softness, actions and little cheep-cheep conversations, and let them walk all over me in spite of their lack of bathroom manners.   It was a short-lived pleasure; as they quickly grew older they weren't quite so cute!

There was the ever-present big cocky white Leghorn rooster who made it his business as boss of the barnyard, self-appointed, to be our wake-up alarm clock every day, way too early in the mornings, standing proudly atop the roof of the chicken house.   Mama at different times had a few other fowl friends there. She sometimes had some Plymouth Rock and Rhode Island Red chickens along with the Leghorns, black and white guinea hens, Bantams, ducks, and turkeys, mostly for the kids' enjoyment, I think.

Big, colorful, strutting tom turkeys with heavy red wattles, their gray and white feathers proudly puffed out around them and their tail feathers spread out into large fans dragging on the ground behind them, were favorites of mine to draw.

On the east/southeast side of the well house and the chicken house was the orchard where we had apple, pear, peach and various other fruit trees, both for canning and for enjoying out of hand.   It was fenced off from the muddy farm pond down a hill to its east.

Across the road to the west from the chicken house, in a yard north of the main house, seemingly a favorite Halloween target for most years, was the wooden 2-seater outhouse with its little moon-shaped cutout window. This important building was relocated often, the pit was filled in with dirt, lime, and gravel, and Dad and the boys dug a deep hole at a new site nearby.

Not far south of that outhouse was the carbide well. Granular carbide was poured into the lined well and, when mixed with water, it produced a gas that was piped underground into the house, smokehouse, garage, well house and the barn for bright, white lighting. Hanging light fixtures in many of the rooms in the house had delicate little white mesh mantels which had to be replaced periodically. We were dependent upon candles, coal oil lamps and lanterns, etc. for other light. Uncle Wayne and Herman Wills, the farmer and relative who lived just north across the fields from us, had carbide lights, too. I don't remember if any others around had them. We just accepted things as they were.

There was a concrete sidewalk from the kitchen porch that ended at the fence at the north edge of the lawn; it changed into a well-worn path to the barn, passing the carbide well and the outhouse.

The house, smokehouse and garage were painted white.

The concrete sidewalk from the main house to the driveway and garage was heavily used and had a variety of cracks and knocked-off corners. It was a good, smooth place for playing with our riding toys that had wheels. It was a perfect place to sit and crack black walnuts and hickory nuts, after bringing them in from the driveway where they had been left to dry and for vehicles to run over them to break up the hulls that protected the nuts' shells. We ate a lot of the nutmeats, and saved more for winter; they were used in cakes, cookies, candy, etc. We did not have pecans or such fancy nutmeats as almonds, pistachios and English walnuts; those were nice surprises later in my life.

The smokehouse was a good-sized, windowless one-story, one-room building with a concrete floor located on the north side of the sidewalk between the garage and the house. At the east side of that room, a stairwell led down to the cellar. After butchering, the meat was placed on long tables on the north side of the room and heavily brined, then covered with layers of butcher paper and cloths. The tables were encased by a fine wire mesh to keep out small animals, flies, etc.

The smokehouse was large enough to be used also for laundry purposes. Dad and the boys relieved themselves back behind the smokehouse and garage buildings. Hollyhocks of all colors stood tall against the front wall of the smokehouse, mingled with trailing green ivy plants.

The garage was across from the house on the east side of the gravel drive. Dad's black iron forge and tools for soldering, horseshoe work, branding irons for cattle and horses, saws, shovels, etc. were kept there along with the lawn mower, gardening tools, and anything else he needed or wanted. When a neighbor needed to have anything mended, repaired, reworked, adjusted, etc., they came to Dad, the fix-it man. Wade, like Dad, was a natural with all tools and, to this day, loves tinkering with repairs and changes in any way connected with any kind of machinery.

This left no room in the "garage", even in the worst weather and even if it happened to be a new one, for the pickup truck Dad drove, which was our family car during all those years; I don't remember that we ever had a sedan when he was alive. Wade was fascinated by the trucks. One morning we found him fast asleep in the seat of a new pickup truck where he had spent the night in his clothes. He has had a pickup all these years.

Cranks were used to start the trucks, cars and tractors, although starters came into use shortly. Farm machinery such as tractors, wagons, hay rakes, etc. were kept in the plot of land behind the barn. My brothers started at a young age to learn how to work with all of these machines and tools.

There was a big lawn surrounding the house. Jake and Wade were responsible for mowing--using the hand-pushed lawnmower--the yard around the house and side yard across the drive. We kept it pretty worn down close to the back door and sidewalks. There were no electric lawn sprinklers and the big red rubber hose we used at an outdoor water faucet became hard and cracked over a short period of time, split from freezing in the winter, and had to be replaced often; we kids used it a lot for spraying each other to cool off and as a replacement for our baths sometimes in the summertime.

Mama didn't plant into pots. Beautiful red rambler roses, pink, white and yellow rosebushes, white lilies, purple flags, white and dark pink peonies, yellow trumpet flowers, etc. had been planted around the house, and other perennial and annual plants were scattered around the yard. Tall flowering bushes such as honeysuckle (which drew honey bees) and spirea bushes with small white flowers were lined up against the front porch and around the outside walls of the house.

There were also many wild flowers to be found. There was a lot of clover for weaving beautiful necklaces (we were always looking for a 4-leaf clover), white Queen Anne's lace, golden rod, fox glove and many bright yellow dandelions in the lawn--we called it the "yard". There were daisies with white petals for playing "he loves me, he loves me not".

There were many mole holes and tunnel runs in various parts of the yard most years. No problem; they, too, were just accepted.

Weeds of all kinds, short ones and tall ones, some with pretty flowers, grew thick in any uncultivated fields, against fences, in roadside ditches, alongside creeks and river beds, under trees in the many old, big thick heavily-wooded forests around (and some that climbed the trees). There were many of these trees, ready to be felled to be used for heat in the homes around. We kids did not play in these forests, not knowing just what wild animals would be living in them, standing and staring at us, ready to pounce. We also had to look out for poison ivy and poison oak. Rocks of all sizes and shapes were lying around everywhere in the fields.

At a young age, I wanted to surprise my mother one day and picked what I thought were beautiful lacy white flowers, I put them into a jar of water in the middle of the dining room table and waited for Mama's happy smile. It wasn't a happy smile at all that I received; I was crestfallen when Mama quickly took them outside and threw them away. Then she hugged me and told me that I had picked "chigger weed". She gave me a little more information about plants that were poison in some way, such as poison ivy and poison oak, and those that might be found in the barnyard, in the fields, etc., even some of them with parts that were edible.

There were tall weeds called cockle burrs that grew rampantly in some of the fields; it was almost impossible to avoid them when walking through the fields. They had small gray, sticky burrs that seemed to jump out at us and they clung to our clothing, especially to our socks, to the point that we could hardly remove them. We laboriously picked them off, or tried to scrape them off with the edge of a knife. Any that were left even went through several washings, sometimes with little harm done to them. After a few bad experiences, we were very careful not to get them in our hair where they had to be cut out with a scissors.

I sat down in the big lounge chair in the living room, closed my eyes and sighed. It had been a busy spring morning and early afternoon. Debbie and I had been planting my flowerpots on the decks and around the house, after spending quite a bit of time at a couple of nurseries picking out the flowers we wanted. Nowadays I pick fewer plants and those that take less time and care. John and I had put in more shrubs and permanent plants in our yard as we grew older, but it is still a time-consuming job to do the flower pots.

I wished now for some sunshine and a good rain in a few days. It is certainly worth the work when the flowers bloom and smell so good in the summer months. I have a couple of neighbors that like to exchange blossoms occasionally.

THE LAND AROUND

THE COUNTRYSIDE AROUND US HAD gentle rolling hills and there were many rocks on the farm. Our acreage did not include any steep, mountainous Ozark hills or cliffs such as those found further south that might cause a rollover. Dad taught the boys to be very respectful of the land and of the machinery they used--no standing in front of or riding as an extra on the tractor with anyone but Dad. They were careful around all machinery and around the animals, too.

Every year at planting time, the tractor and attached rake were used to move to the sides of the fields at the fencerows the rocks of all sizes, some very large, that "came to the top" of the fields; sometimes they were the fencerows. We kids knew to stay away from them because, in addition to harmless bugs and small animals, there probably were snake families and other varmints living there! Our relative/neighbor Herman Wills killed a black wolf in a nearby thicket; there were also foxes, grey wolves, and many coyotes, heard howling and seen mostly at night.

One blustery, cold winter day my brothers and a few of their do-anything buddies accidentally set fire to a very old abandoned two-story house--owned by Grandpa Fulton-- on the Soggy Place just south of us where they had taken shelter, AND because of their busy, natural curiosity. That parcel of land originally owned by John Wesley Fulton was later sold by Grandpa John.

The floor had rotted out in many places, and ground hogs had the run of the place as they made their homes in holes they dug out in the dirt below; skunks and snakes had also taken up residence there. Hoping to smoke the animals out, the boys made small fires in some of the holes in the floor, using old dry used lumber they found inside the aging building, and it all got away from them, burning the building down. Luckily, they weren't hurt.

On many occasions they threw rocks at the old unused, decaying Blue Point schoolhouse near Woody Cave and finally broke out almost all the windows that were left in it.

I don't remember what their punishment was for such misdeeds; it probably was a good spanking and a stern lecture. There were very few "privileges" to be taken away and we weren't confined to our rooms in these instances. I guess we were just supposed to feel ashamed of doing any wrong to anyone or anything and were expected to refrain from a repetition or anything similarly destructive. These "accidents" weren't planned; they just seemed to happen to us.

For a very different kind of thrill, the boys and their friends lowered themselves by rope down into a windmill well on the lower place that was used to pump water into a big round tank for the cattle and horses. They took a flashlight down with them and about 30 feet down into the well found the underground river that ran under the farm. Jake said the well was about 30" or so in diameter, roughly lined with rocks that had been cleared to make short ledges to use for "steps". Depending upon the amount of rain that had fallen, the stream could be a few inches or possibly a few feet deep. The "lower place" was on a level many feet lower than that of the home we lived in.

The stream leads to Woody Cave in Christian County, a few miles south of our farm. The cave's entrance is reported to be about 50 feet high and 100 feet wide, and about 80 feet above Finley Creek. Annabelle tells us stories about the many good times she and "the whole kit and caboodle" had as children on their family picnics at Woody Cave. She tells how intensely beautiful it was with its shallow, layered limestone top that was covered and surrounded by beautiful oak, maple and other trees.

Its tall, wide arched mouth towered above a large level river bed of huge flat stones made smooth as silk by the constant flow of the roaring icy-cold stream fed in flood times by overflowing creeks and sink holes further upstream. There were many stalactite deposits resembling icicles hanging from various points of the cave's ceiling, just above the stalagmites formed below them by their constant dripping of the calcium carbonate.

Nearby, too, were Roaring River State Park, and Lindenlure, a small resort used often, mainly by families for holiday occasions.

When there were heavy rainfall runoffs or quickly melting snows, muddy streams raced through the deeper valleys and ditches in the nearby fields. We were warned repeatedly not to go near them; there was danger of sliding down the slippery muddy slopes into the deep, raging waters and being swept away.

That winding unnamed underground stream started somewhere far northwest of us. It ran under fields and under the hollow of the gravel road from our house to the mailbox a quarter-mile away to the east and continued many miles to the south and southwest into the many caves. Most of the farmhouses and their outbuildings in that area were built higher up on the hills in order to escape possible flooding.

The road north of us from Springfield to Rogersville, a rough, gravel U.S. Highway 60, was very hilly and it was sometimes flooded in many places. I shall never forget one of the years we had so much rain. The hollows for miles around us were flooded; muddy water coursed through fields, over roads, and into farmyards, taking several days to subside enough that the roads could be used. Animals were left standing on the tops of hills where they had instinctively taken refuge.

This was one of the many times we were almost stranded between flooded hollows. I was watching as Dad put on his black hip-high rubber waders. He stabbed a long steel pole into the ground in the middle of the water standing in the field next to the road leading to the mailbox. When the water was released it rushed down into that underground river; I was so frightened that Dad would be swept away in it!!

For a long time after that, when it was my turn to go to the mailbox (R.F.D. #2 - Rural Free Delivery) at that quarter-mile corner, I ran through the hollow as fast as I could. We didn't get much mail. There was very little advertising sent by mail then, but on an average of once or twice a year I was rewarded with an envelope containing a sample stick of Wrigley's gum! I've never had anyone else confirm having received a treat this way. One of my friends says Mama put it in there. Nope. I don't believe Mama was that devious, nor did she have the time to walk to the mailbox.

There are several potential sinkholes all along the land above that underground river, inactive until there is a heavy rainfall. Downhill from the orchard and the barn was the pond. One day when I was picking fruit in the orchard, I heard a big, loud "swoosh" and looked up in time to see the pond disappearing with its fish and turtles, a few piglets and a small calf dropping into the ground--another big sinkhole! I yelled. Dad and the hired help heard the noise and they, along with the "boys", were also yelling and came running to see what had happened. It took several men, ropes and a pickup truck to pull out the horse that was mired there.

The farmers filled the sinkholes in the fields, depending upon their depth and width, with boulders, logs, old tractor tires, old machinery and junk or trash of any kind available, then covered it all with dirt, bushes, tree branches and rocks and leveled it off. This worked until it all sunk in a bit and the next really long, hard, steady rainfall hit, churned in the hole and carried the junk off. Some thought the main stream of the underground river branched off into smaller streams that exited less dramatically in widely scattered places. It is unknown what happened to all the trash, etc. that had been picked up along the way; somewhere it lies underground........

My brothers and their friends played in the sinkholes many times in dry weather. Not long ago Barb told me that she and her girlfriends--Mary Alice and Dixie, mostly--enjoyed playing in them sometimes and played once in the pond. They were completely covered with sticky, stinky brown mud when Mama caught them there and paddled Barb all the way to the house for a hose-off and sent her muddy friends home to be dealt with by their mothers. Barb laughs about it now.

My friends and I mostly stayed out of this kind of trouble; no dirty ponds or sink holes for us! We played on the porch or in the yard with dolls and paper dolls and sometimes sneaked Mama's clothes out and dressed up. We did join the boys in scrub ball games many times or in any of the yard games. Bonabeth, Rheba Nell, Ruby and Gertrude were always around or I was at their homes, but we were in no way very wild. Franny and her friends wouldn't have enjoyed that mess either.

There were no restrictions in the country on burning old buildings, trash, fallen trees, brush, etc. to clear the land.

Hopefully, farm people were responsible enough that they did their burning when there was no wind, in safe places at safe times, and away from buildings and vegetation.

OUR ANIMALS

JOHN AND I WATCHED A good movie on television one evening that was filmed on a farm similar to what ours had been. I found myself thinking of the great childhood we kids had had in and around the barn and animals.

Besides the many other animals we took for granted on the farm, we had our faithful old "speckely" gray mare. We saddled and rode Old Bessie almost every day in warm weather. Sometimes three, four or five of us at a time rode without the saddle, hanging onto each other; if one fell off, we all went, falling into a heap, lying there laughing so hard we hurt! We rode mostly barefoot; we certainly had no need for boots with spurs; Old Bessie went wherever we guided her by the reins or with our heels, and saddled as fast as we wanted; she was the perfect "pet" and I have to believe that she really loved us in her own way. We were constantly hugging and currying her and saw that she was fed and cared for.

Dad at one time had in the stalls six beautiful, tall, shiny, black horses that had been broken to saddle perfectly. Many times his friends came from town and rode them with him. He, and sometimes the boys, rode them to check out the fences and other conditions on the farm, and just for fun, too. One day when Weldon was a toddler, he playfully ran under Dad's favorite saddle horse, Rex. On command from Dad, Rex stood perfectly still until the child was removed. We rode saddle horses quite often through the fields and in the roads.

The boys helped Dad wash them down, curry and brush them. There were some other horses we could ride, but they didn't all saddle; a plain trot is not a comfortable ride and it is tiresome to post all the time in a saddle, even with its stirrups.

There were two large, sturdy, tall black mules that, in addition to important things such as everyday chores, pulled the hayride party wagon for us and our friends and relatives. One of them could open the gate and get them out. The neighbors knew they belonged to Dad and they were returned soon after, along with any cattle they may have set free.

There was a beautiful brown, grey and white spotted Shetland pony we all loved and rode a lot, and a stubborn black jenny (female donkey) we could ride if we could hang on under tree limbs, clotheslines, up against walls and fences (most likely we fell off from laughing so hard.) We gave her a good workout many, many times. I think she disliked us a lot and didn't consider herself to be family or one of our playmates, as Old Bessie did.

In the springtime, Dad would go away for a day or two and leave the chores in the hands of Jake and Wade with help from the other kids. In a short time we would see a big livestock truck back up into the ditch by our grassy side yard, which made a perfect unloading dock for what was to come. We waited anxiously for the back gates of the truck bed to open; it was an exciting time for us all. Occasionally, it was farm machinery, maybe a new big rake or the like. A couple of times it was a new Farmall tractor.

At other times, it would be animals, perhaps beautiful horses or Hereford cattle being unloaded, sometimes it was pigs (maybe Arkansas razorbacks); it might be a load of sheep or goats, maybe skinny Texas longhorns to be fattened up. Nothing surprised us. Dad, Jake and Wade and the truck driver, with a little help from us other kids, would herd the animals up the drive to the barn. At selling time, it was a reverse procedure. The boys also liked joining the men in any branding that was being done.

Sometimes on these trips Dad brought home to Mama big boxes and sacks of bolts, yards and remnants of materials for her use in making our clothes, and sometimes there were large quantities of thread, trim and buttons. He was so proud of himself. I do remember the times he brought home large loads of such things, but made the mistake of coming home a little too happy from the liquor he had consumed that day. That did not make Mama happy!

In addition to the cattle, horses and mules, we also raised sheep, goats, hogs and all kinds of poultry. Shearing sheep was fun, and very different from anything else we did. The sheep were rounded up in the barn and shoved one-at-a-time through a narrow trough. Two of the men caught them and held the frightened animals still while another man used huge manual shears to trim off their wool, which was thrown into a large, tall burlap tow sack.

One man at a time stood inside the sack and stomped the wool down to pack it tightly; his skin became very soft and slick. He was completely covered with lanolin, and even had a hard time washing it off. The big sacks of wool were taken to the town market to be sold. Mama did not have a loom.

We all helped Dad feed the cattle, taking turns throwing down green cornstalk silage from the two big silos at the sides of the barn that had been filled earlier in the summer, pushing it with big black metal shovels down and around the wooden feeding troughs, adding whatever supplement was called for that day, such as cottonseed oil. Putting up silage into the silos was another big job requiring hired hands and labor traded with other farmers. On a few occasions the men threw their straw hats into the silage shredder just for fun.

Riding horses was one thing; riding other animals was another. My brothers and their friends and sometimes Barb and her friends also rode the cows, some of which merely stood still and kept chewing their cuds; some turned their heads around to see what was going on and others ran a little to try to rid themselves of these big burdens on their backs. A big "Moooo" and a tail-switching didn't seem to do any good against their riders, though their tails did smart a little on the girls' bare legs! You could talk to a cow all day and she wouldn't do any more than stare, chew, and switch her tail!

Calves were smaller and much friskier, which made them more fun to ride. Pigs were more of a challenge; they trotted around pretty fast, squealing their displeasure and objections, and there was nothing to hold onto with their short, stiff, slick hair, which was sometimes matted with wet or dried mud. A sow with new pigs was strictly a no-no! Sheep at least had some wool to grab. Goats went crazy, running, bucking, turning. It was very cheap entertainment if you didn't mind scratches and bruises.

The animals just stood around through sunshine, heat, wind, dust, rain, snow, sleet, and storms; occasionally they would lie down for a spell. They gathered in small or large groups most of the time; sometimes a loner stood nearby.

Horses stood next to each other many times, head to rear, so that they could shoo the huge, persistent horseflies off each other with their switching tails, and cows did the same. All they really needed was a good feeding trough, lots of grass, and something to drink. They did have on their wool or hair coats, God-given protection from the elements, and they went through a shedding period in the spring. Every farmer had to have at least one pond for his herd to "stand in and drink from".

There was a cacophony of animal noises most of the time, especially early in the mornings as they joined in the farm wake-up call. Who knows what the animals think about seasonal changes? Who knows what they think about anything???

Their social life was nil, except for the horses. Saddle horses were the luckiest socially of the animals; they were fed, brushed and groomed regularly. They traveled through the countryside carrying their owners in leather saddles and colorful blankets, wearing pretty decorative bridles, horseshoes, and seeing new territory, walking through cool streams and on soft dusty roads. They didn't seem to be displeased. We kids often got to see a horse being "broken" for riding. Some of the young neighbor men could do it.

Weldon (who else?) had many scary, sometimes funny, experiences in the barn and with the animals. He was usually running from or falling off a cow or a calf or a goat or a sow or something. He fell over every possible thing in the barn; he fell over the threshold boards between the rooms or anything else a half-inch tall that stood in his way and he always just laughed. He has a ladder of scars on his nose, scars on his chin, elbows and on his legs. One of the scars was caused by a run-in with a pig when he was four years old.

One day we heard him yelling near the storage house just down the road and saw him running around and around a small tree, being chased and butted by a mad new-mama cow. He had found her and her new calf in a ditch and picked up the calf because he thought it would be better off if brought closer to the house and barn. He broke off all the limbs he could reach to hold onto, and she had him down at one time, standing over him with a couple of her feet somewhere on his body.

At first everybody laughed, but ran to help him when we realized that he really was in trouble, almost too late! He was a bloody mess, having lost most of his shirt, and was bruised, cut and scratched all over. Mama cleaned him up and dressed his wounds with iodine and clean white sheet bandages. He had many, many close calls later wherever he went in his life and still has aches and pains as souvenirs.

At one time Dad hired an American-Indian man to help with the crops and the chores; he and his family lived in the little house down the road before it became the storage house. His young children attended grade school with us. He was paid a small salary in addition to free rent. I never knew how Dad found him.

He was fierce in his loyalty to Dad. He was standing nearby one day when Mama took an icicle from the porch overhang, threw it and hit Dad, bringing a small amount of blood just above his eye. This man came to immediate attention ready to fight Mama until Dad convinced him she was just playing. Mama was very careful around him after that, but she continued giving him and his family vegetables from her garden, fruit from the orchard and plenty of meat and chickens.

He and his family didn't live there very long, just through one season of helping Dad with farm chores.

CARS and TRUCKS

Transportation was a sometimes thing. In that big old red first barn was a beautiful long sedan (was it a Packard, or was it a Nash?), dark blue with a black cloth top, leather upholstery--just sitting there since Grandpa John got sick and died. It was covered with what was called a canvas tarp. Sometimes we lifted the heavy cover and peaked in at the car. We were forbidden to touch it. Now, I have no idea what happened to it; I know it was gone when the barn burned.

Dad always had a pickup truck for hauling things around the farm. After a quick cleanup of the truck, each kid got to take a turn going to the big town of Springfield with Mama and Dad, one a week usually, when we were very young. A wondrous place it was, with bright lights, sidewalks and stores with all kinds of treasures in them. AND we got to buy a real ice cream cone! Mostly, ice cream and candy were made at home, and only occasionally. We had very small stores, Mentor and Pembiney, close to home for small every day purchases.

Sometimes, as a special treat, all of us kids were loaded at the same time into the back of the pickup to be taken to Springfield, which was about twelve miles away over those hilly dirt roads and a stretch of pavement near town. There were wooden side rails on the pickup bed, so we kids could stand up to see the sights. The one big drawback to that was the fact that we were invading the territory of the "BUGS". It didn't take us long to sit back down. In the summer time it was a dusty ride; in the winter, it was a cold one requiring heavy coats and gloves and lots of blankets. None of this mattered--it was an exciting, rare trip to town!!

There was the time we were following a car on the Cotton Gin Hill; the driver was an elderly man traveling at a snail's pace with his wife in the front seat with him. Dad crept up behind the car, bumper to bumper, and pushed the car up that hill at a speed that those nice people couldn't believe. The driver looked to be fighting every control that his car had. Dad released him at the top and passed him; we kids were laughing out loud, but I suspect each of us was just a little bit uneasy--fifteen miles per hour was a little fast under the circumstances.

Dad also thought it was great fun to tease us by turning the headlights off when we passed a small pond. Many times the lights would go off on their own, too, perhaps after Dad hit a big bump, which was a little frightening.

We were especially excited on the few occasions when Dad and Mama loaded us all into the back of the pickup truck and took us for long Sunday trips around our part of the country. He drove over a scary one-way rickety wooden bridge where the tires rode on narrow strips of wood. The bridge was short enough that we could see if a car were waiting at the other end to come across. We could see between the strips the tumbling clear waters of the stream below us; it wasn't called Roaring River for nothing! That bridge is still there, although it has had considerable work done on it. A few one-way bridges are still standing near Ozark, Mo.

A few of our day-long trips with our packed lunches were taken down into the Ozark Mountains south of us on steep, winding, narrow gravel roads through the thick forests; gravel-bottomed streams were rushing swiftly along way down below in the gorge at the bottom between the steep sides of the hills. There were no high bridges or overpasses; Dad drove carefully down those hills into the valleys alongside the streams.

Sometimes we took a home-packed streamside lunch, skipped stones, and waded in the cool water, then loaded up for the trip back home, possibly by a different route. A day-long trip then was not what it is now. One of our trips took us on a raised narrow strip of road through what appeared to be a huge lake, lots of water on both sides; I've racked my brain trying to figure out where we could have been; I was scared to death. WATER!!!!!

Our pickup truck was a very important piece of our lives. I don't remember how often we had new or different ones. Dad not only hauled us around in it, he also used it every day for general hauling around the farm. It didn't always smell like roses, and sometimes it was caked with mud. I recall the time the right window was broken out and he put in a big piece of heavy cardboard until he could get the glass replaced, which seemed like a long time to a girl just beginning to worry about how things looked to other people.

The gas pedal stuck one time when I was driving the kids to the grade school. I turned off the key just in front of a big tree on the edge of the schoolyard after leaping through some ruts and ditches. One day Jake was driving us to a high school function and hit a skunk head-on. That wonderful smell lasted a long time.

EVERY DAY DAYS

IT WAS HOT, HOT AND humid in the homes, hot in the churches, in the schoolhouses and in the stores. It was hot in the yard, the cars and trucks, hot in the barn, hot and dry in the fields, hot and dusty everywhere during the peak of most of the Missouri Ozark summers in July and August. Even any daytime or evening breeze was hot and nearly useless. Many times we slept outside in the yard on old quilts and blankets. There were few noises to break the peaceful quiet except for those made by the farm animals and by tree limbs, swishing leaves and rustling bushes.

The worst of these times was during any of the drought years when almost all of the crops were lost. There were years when our little part of the world was enveloped in choking, blinding, dark clouds of fine, brown dust blowing off the plowed, barren fields. The farmers watched helplessly and hopelessly and the women coped with washing, ironing, dusting and sweeping with no lasting results for weeks and weeks, awaiting the much-needed rain to come.

There were no air-conditioned cabs on the tractors for the comfort of the men driving them, just a hot wind, and a hot sun beating down on top of their straw hats, on their shoulders and on their backs. Girls in knee-length dresses had an advantage over the boys in long bibbed overalls, but the "younguns" wore short pants, sometimes called "rompers". We all did have short sleeves and were barefoot.

Only an occasional cool breeze passed through the yard in the evenings; doors and windows were screened and were left open to catch that breeze. We certainly knew nothing back then of air conditioning, and what few fans we had were small battery-run or handheld and hand-worked! Some hand fans were accordion pleated and had pretty designs, mostly oriental, on them. Many women used these pretty fans during the church services.

We had beautiful blue skies for most of the spring and later summertime days, with white, lazy, fluffy clouds, and mostly starry, moonlit balmy nights. I loved watching those clouds moving around in the blue skies. They were ever-changing; at times I saw faces, always different, some round and fat, some skinny, some with lots of hair, some none. I saw big ships in some clouds, soldiers marching, all sizes and shapes of animals--mostly fish, or cats and dogs, some chasing others.

I still love to watch white clouds--from our back yard, from a car window or wherever they can be seen. I feel that's almost on a par with watching beautiful sunsets or full moons.

We could see a spring/summer storm rapidly approaching our farm from many miles away to the southwest. There would be tall, dark, ominous clouds with bright streaks of blinding white lightning flashing across and through them to the ground, raising the hair on our arms. Rolling thunder rumbled ever louder as it grew nearer to us, bringing with it sheets of hard-driving rain. Mama herded us all inside, even from the screened-in porch, when the storm crossed over Uncle Wayne's pasture across the road and blocked out our view of the cornfield and the forest on the south.

The wind whipped up thick clouds of brown dust from the fields it crossed in advance of the rain and the windows had to be closed. We could smell the dust, then the wonderful freshness of the rain. Many times there were heavy, strong winds and ear-splitting thunderclaps; sometimes the storm gentled off and we could sit on the porch in our chairs and enjoy its cooler temperature and the sound of rain dripping from the eaves.

If it happened to be a soft gentle rain with no lightning, we were allowed to play outside in it. After a big storm had passed our farm, Mama allowed us to run out barefoot to slide in the wet grass or run and splash on the sidewalk and "rassle" in the puddles. The rough gravel drive was not tempting! The warm, bright sunlight that followed was a welcome pleasure.

There were times we went to the cellar due to storms. We had no radio or TV warnings, no sirens. Southwest Missouri and the area for miles around it had many storms and tornadoes back then, as now, a fact that was dreaded every year, but we were lucky never to have had one come close to us.

Because the land immediately around us was fairly level, we could see when a possible tornado was crossing the farms way to the southwest of us, dark and menacing and close enough to scare Mama. She guided us down into the small, dark, dank cellar as Dad watched the storm. Luckily for us and our neighbors, one particular storm we watched was small; it traveled west and north of us, lifted soon, and not one of our neighbors was hurt and very little damage was done to their land or possessions. It brought a good rain and fresh air to us.

Rains were so important to the farmers; they filled the ponds, streams and creeks, nourished the crops, and also filled the rain barrels. We did not have the sophisticated watering systems seen now on farms. Drought years were terrible times for the farmers back then: No rain, no crops--sell the livestock.

There was little traffic, and only occasionally did we spot airplanes flying over our land. They seemed both high in the sky and low enough for someone to see us wave; we yelled and waved frantically at them but never saw a wave returned! Trains, too, were a novelty to us--no tracks in our neighborhood; we saw very little of them in town. We did not see many large transport trucks until Highway 60 was paved; even then they were few and far between.

The noises at our windows were those made by the wind and rain, perhaps thunderstorms--not a wild animal trying to get in. There just wasn't much for us to fear when we slept. We didn't even think of being scared by bumps and noises in the middle of the night. They had a 90% chance of being made by Jake and Wade in their upstairs bedroom; perhaps one of them was taking up too much of their bed. Maybe they were just scuffling as they did so much of the time wherever they were. If a child cried out, comfort came quickly in the form of a series of soft, gentle pats by Mama.

Robbers, thieves and "mean men" were story people, not real to us. We were not afraid of strangers driving or riding by on our road during the day or that someone was lurking in the fields nearby. There were no grizzly stories, real or imagined, on TV--there was no TV. Scary stories on the radio were two things: Not likely to happen to our family way out in the country, and pretty much far out with ogres, witches, etc.

Some nights, though, the moon shone through a bedroom window or door and cast shadows on the wall near me. Maybe one looked like a man or a huge animal. I lay stiff and still in my bed, not moving, eyes wide open, not sleeping, unsure, just waiting quietly for it to move or go away. Then I slept.

My only recurring nightmare was the one where I was being chased by a strange man in dark clothing carrying a "Luger" gun. He chased me through an unfamiliar yard, through fields and into a large barn-like building stacked high with hay bales. I clambered up to the top of those bales, jumped from one to another and slid down the sides away from him, just to have to climb again, over and over. I always awakened just when he was about to catch me. I never have figured out where that came from. A LUGER? What did I know of a Luger???? Why would the man want to shoot me????

It would have been very easy for someone to walk in and rob our home, rob our mailbox, steal our livestock, shoot our dog, but it didn't even cross our minds at all that it might happen. We did not live in fear for our lives and had no arsenal of weapons for defense of body and property. We had no cash, valuables, jewelry, or antiques lying about or hidden under beds. Dad's rifle and shotgun were strictly for his hunting adventures. I still don't have any idea what "robbed us blind" means. Neither did we hear of "crimes of passion" or rapes.

Everybody waved at everybody else when riding by in a car or on a horse; we knew the people for miles around us, where they lived and who their kinfolks were. I recall only the one one-blast shotgun fight between nearby neighbors over a concrete boundary post; one man was killed, which sent a shock wave throughout the area; the post is still there. Events at schools and churches and trading help on the farms or helping someone personally kept us all close.

Postage stamps certainly were not costly at 2 to 3 cents per stamp, but very few letters were written. Many that were written have been found long after having been received, tied in bundles with pretty ribbons, and stashed away in boxes in attics. Much of the handwriting is beautiful. We found a few of these in our home, along with some fragile old fancy valentines, to be handled with care.

During "dog days" we kids were warned to keep an eye out for "mad dogs"; we were told that those large dogs were extra strong during the times this illness raged through them. They were said to froth at the mouth and trot down the roads with their heads hanging down, swinging back and forth, and their tails down, red tormented eyes downcast.

If we kids were ever to see one when we were on the road, we were to climb quickly the fence into the pasture and lie down, quiet as mice; supposedly mad dogs never looked up from the road. We were lucky never to have seen one except maybe in a picture, but our imaginations were lively enough to make us aware, and made for some bad, bad dreams. We wondered what could have made them so mad.

We were always, of course, to be aware of the big Hereford bull that might be nearby in that field. Although we never saw him mad, pawing at the ground, etc., we stayed pretty close to the fence. Once in a while, people caught glimpses of ground hogs, possums, wolves and coyotes; we heard them howling at night, too, at the moon, we were told.

BUTTERFLIES, BIRDS, BUGS, BEES AND SMALL ANIMALS

Sometimes it seemed that there were a million beautiful, colorful butterflies, all colors, all sizes--such as the Monarchs, which were my favorites--visiting the blossoms of the flowers and weeds in the summertime. We sat very still, hoping they would land on us. It never seemed fair to me that butterflies were killed and stuck with straight pins in a notebook or shadow box, even for a school project.

There were birds of all sizes and colors that nested in the trees and we went to sleep with the sounds of their tittering and wakened to their cheerful morning songs. Humming birds, robins, wrens, blackbirds, cardinals and mocking birds were favorites, messy sparrows weren't. We kids tried repeatedly to match the calls of the whippoorwills but failed. There were owls, buzzards and crows flying around the fields and barnyard. An ugly black buzzard circling overhead was oftentimes a bad omen that some animal had died in a nearby field.

Quite often, we saw terrapins and toad families, and there were croaking green frogs and large and small turtles in the pond. We could hear the coyotes howling in the forests, somehow a lonely sound, and saw a red fox or a gray wolf occasionally, although they tried to stay out of sight of the humans. The lower place had more and different snakes because that land was so rocky and wasn't as busy. We certainly had no desire to see a rattler or a water moccasin, although small blue racers, colorful garters and black snakes didn't scare us.

There were several insects in the summertime that weren't too much fun. One day Mama looked up from her work in the garden and yelled to all the kids to run into the house, quickly! She instructed us in an almost frantic voice to close all the windows and doors, upstairs and down, and stay inside the house. We could see a very dark undulating cloud in the south across Uncle Wayne's field, moving swiftly in our direction with a loud humming/buzzing sound. In a matter of minutes our house was engulfed in tiny black OAT BUGS. They covered the screens and windows and the outside walls. After awhile, they moved on, leaving their dead behind--a real mess--some even inside the screened-in porch.

Another year, it was grasshoppers; they stripped clean the cornfields, the garden and the flowers. Gypsy moths were leaf strippers, too. Endless numbers of spiders in lovely webs, fleas, mosquitoes, wasps, bumblebees, hornets, dirt daubers, gnats, and ants lived among and around us and there were way too many "stink bugs" and ticks in the forests. Ticks were best removed by hot tweezers before they dug in. Ticks regularly had to be removed from Old Pood, especially from the insides of his ears. I can still imagine the damage done by the seven-year locusts. Big black and yellow "woolyworms" were fascinating to watch, inching along; they were supposed to be telling us by the changes in their colors what kind of weather we would be having later.

There was little defense then against these insects. The animals had enough natural "horse sense" to stand next to each other, opposite ends, using their tails to swish away the huge horse flies around them. Tightly woven screens for windows and doors were a must to keep out the millions of ordinary house flies and mosquitoes; bug sprays for indoor use were not available.

Not all bugs were hated. What we called "June bugs" (because they came in June) were hard-shelled, clean, pretty, shiny, dark green round bugs nearly 3/4" in diameter that were used by kids as "airplanes". Long strings were tied to the tops of their strong legs and they were allowed to buzz around and around our heads until we freed them later.

There was a noisy bug called a cicada; it shed its hard transparent shell onto a tree trunk and we kids used the delicate little shells for "cars". Lightning bugs made beautiful flickering patterns in the night sky; they were stuck onto our fingers and worn as bright rings or several of them were gathered and put together into a pint jar with holes in the lid to make a "lantern", then released later. The 3-inch light brown "walking stick" bug with long crooked "stick" legs and body looked like its name. We had our own honey bees for a few years and tried not to bother their hives, enjoying their end product later.

We just lived every day with these animals and insects all around us. We really didn't worry much about their being there. Were we the intruders or were they? We did not have access to all the bug killers and sprays that are now available; we also didn't have weed killers. It was "do what you can" and welcome the first freeze.

CHURCH, ETC

At an early age, I started going to Center Point Church of Christ with Aunt Ida and Uncle Wayne Scott. Mama was too busy then with kids and homemaking. She later took the other kids to Harmony Baptist Church a few miles away. Dad wouldn't go because he said some of the members came out and stood beside him and "bugged" him to join the church. I understand he did join later when they got a new preacher.

Everyone wore their "Sunday best" clothes to church. Women wore fancy hats, some of which sported long, soft ostrich feathers and colorful ribbons. They wore nice cotton gloves--white in the summer, black in the wintertime--dress shoes, and rayon hose held up with homemade elastic garters. Men wore their dark Sunday suits, hats, gloves and shoes. Shoes, after a few wearings, showed more wear and tear than now. Children were dressed appropriately.

One of my favorite friends, a classmate and teammate, went to the same church; the minute we knew the other was in the room, we started giggling and shaking, trying so hard to be quiet. There were no words spoken nor did we even look at each other. We just couldn't stop--we were almost sick from trying to stop; we even received some frowns and finger shaking from the adults for it a time or two. This went on for what seemed like months.

Her name was Georgia. I enjoyed so much being around her and we visited in each others' homes a lot. I didn't see her after high school graduation; I heard that she married one of our schoolmates. I have just recently learned that she passed away some time ago.

One Sunday morning Uncle Wayne carefully drove us the one-and-a-half miles to church, which is across the road west of the school house. This was after one of the worst ice storms we had ever had. Ice 3" to 4" thick covered everything: The gravel road, fences, tree branches in the forests, bushes, the fields, ponds, barns, houses and their yards. I was fascinated by the beauty of the strong glare on everything it touched around us.

The sun shone as brightly as I've ever seen; it was blinding and we had to squint to see. Uncle Wayne was calm; he had been in similar situations before in his long lifetime; there was no traffic. Attendance that day was way down, though. The attendance figure was always put up in front with large interchangeable wooden number blocks on a wooden 20" square board, showing both the last week's attendance and the current attendance. It was a safe, slow trip to and from church and an unforgettable one for me.

The preacher always led us in our favorite religious songs (still favorites of mine today) which included "The Old Rugged Cross", "In the Garden", "What A Friend We Have in Jesus" and "The Saints Go Marching In". There was no musical accompaniment, there was no choir, therefore there was no choir leader, but we all really belted out loud and clear, good voice or bad. Kids and parents sang together in questionable harmony. I'm sure there were enough good, although untrained, voices on tune to carry the bad ones through the melody--no one complained.

At that church, Sunday school lessons and discussions were started at the beginning of the Bible and each Sunday we started where we left off the week before. Men, not women, led the prayers back then in that church and led the Sunday school classes. There were communion services every Sunday.

I "went forward" at Center Point during the invitational song "Just as I Am" and was baptized in 2 to 3 ft. deep water in the James River in March when I was thirteen; there were several of us that day. The preacher held my nose shut with his fingers as he dunked me under the water. I didn't notice how cold and muddy the water was. Mama had made me a new dress; it was a sodden mess and so was my hair, but I had such a wonderful feeling that it just didn't matter.

Barb was supposed to be baptized in December when she was thirteen, but that was at the time Dad died. She and Mama were baptized together in the James River into Harmony Baptist Church later the next spring. My other brothers and sisters were also baptized into Harmony Baptist Church as they grew older.

Mama was calm but adamant when she told me that, in order to be lady-like (which she explained was my goal), I should always keep my knees together, skirt hem pulled down over my knees, especially when sitting or lying down, as in the yard, etc., and even when walking. I've made that a habit ever since, and it seems as if most women my age, at least, do the same, even when wearing slacks; certainly the majority of men do not seem to have this compulsion.

She was also adamant when she told me never to pick up a dirty handkerchief I might find in the road or in the schoolyard, etc. but never gave me a reason that made sense. I remember finding one on the road to the mailbox one time, but walked on by it as if it were poison. What a waste of a good handkerchief Dad could have used.

I understood there were "dirty" words we were not to say, but we weren't given many of the words. Our bodily functions were not to be discussed, nor were the words used as epithets. I knew we weren't supposed to talk about our periods, or use God's name in vain (whatever that meant). We did not run around naked.

I was walking home from grade school one day in a group that included some new, older boys in our school; one of them mumbled; I think he was asking me if I wanted to do something. He was sorta leering (at least I thought it might be leering, but what did I know) and his friend was snickering, so I decided it was not something I wished to do and I walked quickly ahead.

Innocence was so pronounced that we didn't really know when some words and suggestions were bad, and didn't know what they meant! I don't hesitate to say that I wish it were still that way. I know Jake and Wade found out about the "bad" words long before I did. I know some of them now--in this day and age, they're everywhere and it's hard to ignore them--but I won't say them. I think Mama is looking down on me and she and God wouldn't like to hear me say them.

As a matter of fact, I personally don't like to hear anyone say them and know many people who feel the same way. They can ruin a party conversation or a good movie or TV show for me in a hurry.

FUN AND GAMES

I WAS WORKING ON A TRIP to Colorado that John and I were planning with friends, to be taken in a couple of weeks. We would drive to some familiar places and to many new ones. We had always enjoyed the company of these particular people and had spent so much time with them in years before.

There were no vacations planned back where I was a child; farmers worked hard every day. There were chores that had to be done. Any time away was maybe for a funeral out of town or such, and plans were made for help at home. We never heard of going to the seashore or to an island, to the mountains, back East, out West, to Florida, etc. Seashores, mountains and islands were geography assignments in school, to be found on a map or a globe or in a textbook.

Only the youngest babies took naps, which probably were small vacations for Mama. I imagine she was glad to see school start, which got us away for a while, and gave us homework to keep us busy in the evenings.

Dad and his friends and buddies had quail, duck, coon, rabbit and other hunting in the woods and back forty fields and forests with their birddogs, and sometimes fishing, playing pool, etc. The bird dogs treed the animals or birds and stood at attention, pointing until called off by their "masters". Dad had both a rifle and a shotgun.

One of our doctors, Dr. Wills, came to join him and others many times. They carried duck calls and were careful to wear their red caps and stylish flannel-lined waterproof hunting jackets with the roomy game pockets inside and out. They did have one minor shooting accident when they went out with a man who had never hunted before and didn't pay attention to the rules Dad laid down. He was okay, but frightened a little. The boys were not old enough to be allowed to go on these hunts. They did, though, have their own possum and rabbit traps to tend.

Mama did not have her own personal sport to enjoy. On occasion she and Dad went to the nearby very small "business district" of the rural community of Mentor and played croquet in the little park there with other adults. The children got to watch, or we could run around the park, enjoying its swings and slides, or playing tag, etc. with other children there.

We kids always had something to play besides the usual "tag" games; we played the old favorite hopscotch on the sidewalk, played jacks, and played mumblety-peg with Dad's heavy pocket knife (he used it sometimes to whittle out shapes of animals, trees, etc. for us.) We had a few individual jump ropes and a long heavier rope to be held by two people, one at each end, so that more than one person could jump at the same time.

We skipped smooth, flat, round stones on the ponds and rivers; we chinned ourselves on low-hanging limbs or hung by our knees; we walked on our hands; we tried to see who could make the most somersaults at a time; we played leap frog. This was very inexpensive entertainment. I had a favorite tree not far from our house where I could go off by myself to sit, lean against its gray/black bark trunk, and read.

Dad hung a huge used tractor tire on a sturdy rope to a big limb of one of the old oak trees in the yard; this was in addition to the regular long rope swing with its wooden seat that he made for us, hanging from a limb of another tree. We climbed the trees. I fell from one of them when the limb I was standing on broke off. I landed flat on my back, and was knocked breathless for a short time, gasping for air, and saw a zillion stars; I could see and hear but couldn't move or call out. I was reminded of this feeling many years later when I fell hard, flat on my back, while snow skiing.

We tunneled holes large enough to crawl into at the bottoms of big dry haystacks; we played on the tops of the stacks, and we slid down their sides, well aware of the itching it would bring us later.

We played a game called "holes" in the tramped down bare dirt of the yard adjacent to the sidewalk at the house. For this game, we each had our own favorite marble we called a "taw" which we shot from our palms with our thumbs for each of five holes including the one where we had started and returned to, progressively, the game plat dug in an L-shaped triangle. Fewest shots won. The boys usually won this game.

Mama and Dad learned early on that our yelling was for fun or annoyance with each other; screaming could be because of pain from cuts, bruises, bites, fear of danger or anything that really scared us.

During most of the spring and summertime, we were barefoot. When school started in the fall, our feet were tough as leather, but we still could feel the stobs and stickers we stepped on. We had many painful scratches, bruises, cuts and scars. We did get to be very dirty sometimes, there was so much dust, then mud after a rain. Bring out the hose!

Farm kids were not overly sick; I think we were immune to many germs after a while. Playing outside in the yards and schoolyards in fresh, unpolluted air with friends and relatives was undoubtedly a big plus for our future health and well-being. We couldn't know how polluted the air around us would be in future years because of man's well-meant, wonderful work-saving inventions and discoveries.

Jake was especially good at walking on his seven-feet tall homemade stilts made from thick tree limbs with smaller limbs or wooden bars attached across them for footpads held up with leather straps. The boys also had BB guns for firing at birds in the trees or tin cans on top of posts, never at each other or the house or our animals, always to be watchful and careful of running kids. Homemade slingshots made from small forked limbs and rubber bands, large for rocks and small for pebbles and paper wads, were a must and we all had small homemade kites.

When the boys were old enough to absorb what he was doing and saying, Dad would take just them and the birddogs hunting with him; this gave him the opportunity to teach them personally the correct ins and outs, especially the safety elements, of hunting birds and animals. Wade is still an avid hunter--mostly quail now, so abundant in the Ozarks.

We had little red metal wagons for hauling our treasures and the smallest kids, and there were several scooters and tricycles. We turned a rain barrel over onto its side and tried to walk it or rolled it around with one of the kids in it. We had a black and white "pet" pig named Oscar that we tried to ride astraddle in the yard but he didn't cooperate well and could run almost as fast as we. He probably rolled his eyes when he saw us coming and thought "oh, no, not again!" If we could get on, he was good at throwing us off with his sharp, unexpected corners; there was nothing for us to hold onto what with his short, stiff hair. He definitely did not like riding in the barrel.

A "whangdoodle" was made from any old piece of junk iron tied to the end of a piece of twine or rope and it was whirled around the head. Weldon was headed for the toilet one day and walked into the space where Wade (who else would it be?) was swinging his whangdoodle; it hit Weldon a glancing blow on the head and made a long cut that required a trip to town for stitches and left a big bump that is still there. Needless to say, Wade got another spanking and a lecture. Many times men came through the country and bought for a very small pittance any old junk iron pieces farmers might have lying around, to be used in the war effort.

Across the driveway there was a side yard south of the garage; we kids begged Dad to have a swimming pool built there; we didn't understand why that was turned down immediately and repeatedly every summer. We and our friends and cousins chose it as a perfect place to play softball later on. The house was hit often, but one year Jake hit a long home-run fly ball that broke the only window on the east side of the second floor of our house. He was both scared and very proud of that feat!

I can barely remember seeing Dad and his male relatives and friends playing softball sometimes at a school function. He really hit the ball a long way and probably would have been a pretty good team player, given the chance. The boys' strong swings and their long running strides as they rounded the bases were like Dad's.

(I laugh to myself now when I think of the many ball games we played later with our kids on our July 4 picnics in Barb and Davy's big back yard. At one of our later games, Davy started us off with a large flag and we saluted and said the Pledge of Allegiance, after which we sang a terribly off-key version of the National Anthem. We adults beat them badly up until a few years ago; we had many years of experience hitting, fielding and running bases, but also had many years of growing older. It was always so much fun, and everybody came prepared with food, fireworks, balls, bats and gloves.

After many years of trying so hard, the kids were ecstatic after they finally won a game against us. This was followed by diving, swimming and loud rough-housing in the pool.)

Snowfalls then were more frequent, whiter, deeper, fluffier, cleaner, and stayed on the ground for a longer time, so perfect for our winter games. They drifted high against the sides of the house and sometimes piled up high on the window sills. When the first snow fell, we were allowed to run barefoot from the sidewalk through the yard to the ditch and back; usually one icy run was enough and we went for our boots. The yard was soon a mess of foot tracks, angel wings, snowmen and results of snowball fights--a place for happy kids. Enough snow fell then to build forts and enough for playing the popular fox-and-goose game, etc.

Clean, fresh deep white snow made wonderful treats, mixed with root beer, jelly, syrup or molasses, etc.

If we ran out of games, we just thought up something! Playing in the ditch between the road and the yard was such great fun, with or without snow. We laid out roads with hills, we used boxes, lumber scraps, rocks and sticks for houses and barns; clumps of grass were haystacks and tall weeds were our trees. We didn't know then that we should be keeping for antiques all those many little cast iron cars, trucks, tractors, etc. that we took for granted and played with constantly.

One day Jake and Wade "buried" one of my dolls in the ditch; her "real" hair and cloth body weren't too pretty after that. They thought it was funny; those boys were as onery as all get-out!

We girls made pretty necklace chains with clover leaves and blossoms, daisies, strands of popcorn and paper links, and we played "he loves me, he loves me not" as we pulled off daisy petals.

When I was very young, I made a playhouse near the henhouse, outlined with rocks. I used old chicken nests from the henhouse for furniture. Baaaad, baaaad move! I did that only once; the nests were full of tiny chicken mites. In a matter of minutes I was fully covered with them--even in my hair. I ran to my mother, crying, yelling and flinging my arms at my head. After she got over her scare, Mama doused me completely with kerosene then gave me a lye soap bath, top to bottom, and the old nests were burned. Another no-no learned the hard way, but with no lasting damage.

Inside games were dolls and paper dolls for the girls, or many times coloring books and Crayolas. For any of us doing personal artwork, we used Big Chief ruled tablets and lead pencils we sharpened with a paring knife or Dad's pocket knife. We played ping-pong, checkers, Chinese checkers, dominoes, jacks, blocks, and puzzles, and the boys brought in from outside summertime-duty their cast-iron toy trucks, tractors and cars to push around on the linoleum floors, making the "car" sound "uddn , uddn, uddn".

To entertain the youngest kids, we made hand silhouettes against the wall. We sometimes made a church by lacing and curling our fingers inside our palms; our thumbs were the front doors. We stuck our forefingers into the air for the steeple, opened our hands and there were the people in the church.

We loved to watch our elders play the card game "Rook", but NEVER ON SUNDAY! Look for church visitors.

Sometimes when Mama and Dad were not home, we turned over the dining room chairs and pushed them around over the linoleum as "cars". We took the feather ticks off our beds and made them into sleds for a bumpy, rough ride down the long staircase, yelling and laughing all the way. A busted one made quite a large cloud of flying feathers which stuck to our hair and sweaty bodies and was a mess to be cleaned up and somehow explained to our parents (they acted as if they had never done such a thing!)

As young kids, Jake and Wade played their boy-games with one another and with friends and/or relatives from neighboring farms. One day our cousin Manuel rode to visit them on his new (boy's) bike with the high bar front-to-back. At that time I had never had a chance to ride a bike; I hadn't even seen one up this close, only in a picture in a catalog. While they were occupied elsewhere, after a stern "don't touch it" lecture from my cousin (he should have known better), I got on the forbidden bike and tried to ride it.

On, off, on, off again. The "offs" were the continuous falls I took one after another and the scrapes I got. I stubbornly kept trying. Finally, I made it to the barn and back, wobbly but no falls, some scratches, bruises, blood and tears and a great feeling of satisfaction and exultation although I knew it was wrong, and I was met by a very, very mad, yelling cousin!

Jake and Wade and cousins and friends spent a lot of time going "froggin". Mama was expected to "fry up" these little frog-leg delicacies after they were cleaned by the boys.

Through their early years my brothers were always together, plotting, daring each other into something that might be forbidden or at least frowned upon. When they were not yet in their teens, they smoked their own version of roll-your-own cigarettes out behind the barn, until they were caught. Often their "cigarettes" were made of corn silk and crushed grapevines, a recipe learned from some older friends. When Dad caught them one day, he made them roll their own from his tobacco tin and little papers and they had to sit down with him, converse, and smoke to the finish. They were more than a little sick and gave up their clandestine smoking for a little while.

ILLNESSES, ACCIDENTS, ETC.

I LOOKED DOWN AT THE BIG blue bruise staring back at me from the upper part of my right arm and I remembered hitting the edge of the kitchen cabinet a few hours earlier. Nothing new here; I bruise easily since I've been on Coumadin, something I have grown accustomed to. I suppose we kids had near a million bruises that were not worrisome and went unnoticed or unexplained. There weren't many hours we weren't into something other than sitting quietly.

There was an occasional boil on one or another of us; Mama lanced boils with a needle she had sterilized in the flame of a match then she touched them up with a dab of iodine or such. That meant a new rash of lectures from her about keeping clean. Mashed fingers and minor cuts were an accepted part of farm life.

We were seldom ill--just the usual run of annoying little things that most kids have. Mama gave us a swig of Vicks to swallow if we had a sore throat (I understand that's a big no-no now) and rubbed it on our chests if the cold happened to be deeper. Sometimes we had a steaming teakettle of water by our bedside, used when we had the croup. Parents were pretty much on their own with winter-time illnesses, what with no neighborhood doctors or hospitals to call on in rural areas, but they learned from experience a lot of what was expected of them in each case, or could call on an older neighbor, preferably one with several kids.

One day young Jake and Wade were chopping trees in the woods, taking turns swinging their axes, across from each other, something they had done before many times with Dad. Something went wrong with their count, and Jake was hit squarely on top of his head, leaving a large bloody gash, but was not knocked out.

Jake remembered being aware that Wade was beside himself, screaming and crying; he ran back and forth several times towards the house, and finally made it to the home of a nearby neighbor named Zula Cowan. Jake was taken first to Uncle Wayne's house where Bert and Annabelle were grinding feed and they called Dr. Wade in Ozark. Jake was then taken to a hospital in Springfield. Mama was in Springfield with Dad at the time, so it was up to me to be "Mama" at home.

Jake still had the inch-plus square dent in his head; I felt it with my fingers when I was down home one day not long ago. Luckily, no damage was done to his brain and he could still give me a hard time. In cases such as this, Mama would mostly wring her hands, walk about in circles and sorta cry out, wailing, you might call it; she hated seeing her babies hurt in any way.

Jake also had scarlet fever and our home was put under quarantine for a few weeks. He was not allowed to come out of the living room where Mama had made a bed for him. To "entertain" him (and us), we made ugly faces at him through the window as we went ahead without him and played our games in the yard outside his room. None of the others caught it, unlike measles, chicken pox and mumps, which made the rounds quickly.

Jake was the one that cut off with Mama's big scissors Barb's eyelashes because "they were too long for her to wear eye glasses if she ever needed them"; he was such a thoughtful brother.

We all had an occasional bout of sprained ankles, stubbed toes, mashed fingers, painful sunburn, a few freckles, and went through the pimple stage. We were like most other kids in that we struggled to wiggle a loose baby tooth enough to pull it out. We placed it under our pillows at night and wakened to see if it had been replaced by the tooth fairy during the night with a bright, shiny nickel or dime.

There were no "shots" given then to ward off chicken pox, measles, mumps, etc.--we just suffered through them. If someone at school came down with them, we all had them; most of us have at least one or two small round chicken pox scars left over. Earaches called for a drop of some kind of warmed oil into the ear, covered with a hot towel, to go with our moaning. It seemed to us that they lasted at least a week or two, but now I don't think they did. There was an occasional stye in the eye or maybe someone got the lovely "pink eye". We had Ex-Lax for helping with constipation, which wasn't often what with all our good food and balanced diet.

Better for us than any medicine was a big folder of hand-drawn "sympathy" or "get well" cards drawn on tablet paper, received from our schoolmates of various ages and talents.

Dr. Wade was it, everything "doctor" except dentist. From his office in "downtown" Ozark, he made house calls in his old black sedan, driving throughout the countryside and smaller towns, carrying in a big black leather bag full of helpful tools, splints, salves, medicines and many other things. He didn't charge much. Sometimes he was paid, oft-times at his own request, with fresh or home-canned fruit or vegetables, a few chickens or a cut or two of fresh beef or pork.

I do remember that Weldon was ill with something that called for a dose of the dreaded CASTER OIL! It took all of us kids to hold him down on the bed and he threw his head back and forth and up and down and Mama liked to never got his mouth open wide enough to spoon it in through his clinched teeth--some ran down his cheeks and neck and into his hair and ears. We were all a little sick at the thought of it and couldn't look--there was no laughing! We all had suffered through a taste of that awful stuff at one time or another. Knowing it had to be done didn't help.

Our many scratches, burns and bug bites were most often coated with Mercurochrome, Unguentine or Iodine. We always had bruises somewhere on us and we used lots of talcum powder for itchy red rashes. Home-made bandages made from old sheets, etc. were used for wrapping when needed--no boxes of handy little prepared bandages then, and no little cotton balls or cotton swab sticks bought at a nearby store. (Mama must have had a million old sheets, always white; they were used for all kinds of things!)

I don't remember any kids that wore glasses then; I wonder now if there weren't many who could have benefited greatly from them.

WORK, WORK, WORK
LOTS OF LAUNDRY

Monday on the farm was our main washday. Mama had a large Maytag gasoline-powered washing machine on wheels on the concrete floor of the smokehouse, along with a big galvanized steel tub on legs she filled with "rinsh" water. A large rubber hose was attached to the bottom of the washer and the other end hooked over the top edge of one side of the washer, let down for drainage later. There was a stainless steel hand washboard kept nearby for ground-in dirt and stains, and hand-powered wringers were part of the washing machine itself.

When we had rain, soft rainwater was collected in large 55-gallon barrels set in just the right places under the eaves of the house to catch the runoff. The water was heated in the wintertime in the kitchen for the washing machine or in the summertime in the big black cast iron kettle kept in place on the east side of the smokehouse.

First, the white and light-colored clothes were washed with a soap Mama had made earlier sometime (many times made with lye) in the big black kettle or with Rinso or Oxydol bought at the store. There were no fabric softeners. Next, medium colors were washed, followed by the darks--all in the same water, with extra soap and hot water added as needed. Everything was made of cotton; there were no rayon or nylon clothes back then and we didn't wear silk, having never even heard of it. Washing was done many other times during the week, too, as there was a lot of it. Mama made her own starch with flour and water; sometimes it was a little lumpy.

Clothes were hung--like things together in a row--by wooden clothespins on the many wire lines Dad had strung from tree to tree in the back yard; they were dried and softened as they fluttered in the breezes of the summertime and by freezing dry in the icy wintertime. If we were in the middle of a blizzard or a rainstorm, there was no washing done that day.

Mama insisted that the dresses and shirts were to be hung neatly by the shoulder seams where they met the top of the sleeves after they had been "flipped" to get some of the wrinkles out; skirts, pants and underwear, etc. were to be hung from the waistbands. Thin cotton handkerchiefs were plentiful as there was no such thing as Kleenex; they were hung by their corners, 2 or 3 together. They were white most of the time; some had fine colored lines on them. Mama had beautiful small lace-trimmed or embroidered handkerchiefs for dress.

I have since seen clothes hung on lines by any part of the garment picked up first, perhaps by a side seam, and any other part picked up next. Mama must be looking down from heaven, shaking her head.

Linens were hung neatly from their corners. There were many sheets, pillow cases, towels, tea towels, table cloths, napkins, etc. We did not have little throw rugs to put in the laundry.

For many years there were lots and lots of diapers to wash by themselves with lye soap and bleach for the doo-doo; each hung separately, corner to corner, to take advantage of the strong sunlight on them. Could diaper rash be traced back to that? Break out the talcum powder in big tins!

Tuesdays were the main ironing days. Ironing was done (a lot of it by me when I was big enough) on the round dining room table which was padded with an old blanket and some sheets. Three flat "sad irons" were heated on top of the stove and used, one at a time with a clip-on holder/handle, until they cooled off, then exchanged for hot ones. When Fran was big enough, she would iron for Barb and me if we would sew for her. (For many of the past several years, she was a seamstress in a men's clothing shop in Springfield, sews beautifully for her daughter and herself and occasionally makes a special shirt for her menfolk.)

When we did get electricity--brought in by the REA (Rural Electrification Administration)--I would iron at that same round table as fast as I could so as not to use too much current, and Barb, Mama and Fran would fold and put away. It was a big improvement over what we had before, but that was one heavy iron!

THE WORK GETS HEAVIER

ALL OF US, EVEN THE little ones, had our own special chores. While I helped mostly with the washing, ironing, cooking, etc., the boys worked outside. The younger kids gathered the eggs, fed the chickens, set the table, straightened up the dining and living rooms, or did whatever they were capable of doing; they didn't have to be told-- most things were automatic after a few times of doing.

My brothers slopped the hogs; they milked the cows, mostly Jerseys, Herefords and Guernseys, and helped with the plowing, planting, cultivating and harvesting of all the crops. They all learned their lessons well; this was learning by doing. These were experiences they would need to fall back on a few years later when Dad died, much too young, leaving our mother with so many young children to raise by herself.

Milking our many cows after one of Dad's buying trips was a family project many years, though. It was done by hand in the evenings in the stalls in the barn and all of us kids learned it at an early age. The hands were wrapped tightly around the teats with fingers turned in to squeeze the teats, top to bottom, for a strong, steady stream. I could hit my brothers with a stream of the warm milk from quite a distance but they could hit me, too! Needless to say, sometimes we came out very, very sticky from those milk fights; it definitely was more fun in the summertime, in spite of the flies. At least we could hose off after! My brothers milked directly into a cat's mouth sometimes. Funny to them; not so funny to the cat when they missed and hit his eyes.

All this waste; we were told that people were starving in Africa. Where or what was Africa?

We milked into aluminum milk pails held between the knees or resting on the ground, which made a pretty loud noise at first, sometimes dull and flat, sometimes with a ringing sound. We and some of our neighbors signed up for dairy pickup in the late 1930's. Most of the milk was poured into 10-gallon lidded aluminum pails inside the well-house for the dairy pickup truck the next day, and we kept what was needed by us. The milk we kept in the small ice box or refrigerator to drink was not pasteurized.

We couldn't miss a night's milking because that would be hard on the cows. If a neighbor were too ill to do his own milking, others pitched in to do it for him, knowing that the favor would be returned if ever needed. Sometimes we had to be aware of a cranky cow that wasn't too happy about the whole thing and she would start us out with a kick or two. When the milking was finished, the milk sat for a short time in our personal buckets and the rich cream was skimmed off; we churned a glossy yellow butter from it and it was also used by Mama in her rich desserts.

Bulls were penned off by themselves most of the time, which sometimes made them cranky, pawing at the ground and snorting. They were turned loose with the herd, including cows, at certain times of the year, which in turn made them happy. Several months later, we had a whole new crop of calves. The cows were pretty blasé about the whole process. Girl calves--heifers--were kept for milking and to enlarge the herd after a couple of years. Boy calves' testicles were castrated ("cut"), which made them steers, to be fattened and sold or butchered for eating later. Male hogs also were "cut". I never learned to like the "cuttings" or "mountain oysters" as they were called for some reason.

Cows and cattle had a way of getting out of the pastures; when that happened at night, they were often found a few miles away the next day and were returned to the owners. Sometimes some of our animals were branded by Dad and neighbors when they were brought to our farm. Men on horseback, with the help of their birddogs, rounded up cattle, sheep or hogs and herded them into wooden fenced-in pens in the barnyards where they were held, then run one at a time into a long narrow chute and picked out at its end for butchering, branding, shearing or selling, etc.

Farmers were always mending their fences. Some of the fences were made of barbed wire spaced to keep the cattle and horses from getting out. Others were made of a closer wire mesh fencing to keep small animals inside the fields, but had at least one strand of barbed wire on top. Often fields were outlined with log rail fences. Some of the "richer" farmers had miles of upright wooden slat fences painted white--not too much of this in our part of the country. A few fences were kept in better condition and were neater than others.

Many farmers, during the lean years, could not afford to paint even their white houses and red barns until they had a more profitable year later.

I thought hay baling/binding time was fun when I was a young kid; I got to ride around and around in the saddle on the mule that was harnessed to the hay baler. I think now that the men were probably tickled to death to have a "pijun" like me to prod that mule to keep going! They bragged on me to Dad and made me feel very important. Threshing time and shocking wheat were messier, and making haystacks with a pitch fork was an "itchy", dirty job.

Cornfields were planted in a checkerboard pattern; you could see down each row in several directions; it was much later that it was planted by a drill in long thick rows, and most of it was open pollinated. The cornstalks were very tall. Having a feel for east or west and north or south directions was important in a forty-acre field thick with mature corn. On a cloudy day with no direction from the sun, it would have been easy to turn the wrong way and walk across the cornfield away from the edge one wanted.

Farmers picked corn and cut sargo by hand. Depending upon the acreage of corn, they used hired help including relatives and friends, sometimes neighbors, sometimes transients, for many long, hot days of back-breaking labor, rising early in the mornings to do their other chores first.

A team of horses was hitched to the wagon used to collect the ears of corn to be taken to the corn cribs. The men picking corn very quickly worked through many pairs of heavy gloves, sometimes one pair a day as they tore loose the big stiff ears from the corn stalks. It was preferred to do the picking as soon as conditions were right. Cornstalks were made into the silage to be stored in the silos mentioned elsewhere. Mechanical corn pickers came into use later in the 1930s. I got to be pretty good at shucking corn for our meals and cutting out the bad stuff.

After a few sneaked drinks, the men helping with the silo fillings and thrashings sometimes threw their hats through the corn cutters. If the men seemed to be having too much fun, laughing a lot and being loud, even trying to sing some bawdy songs, Mama went to see what was going on. If she found them drinking and being a little reckless, she took what was left of their whiskey and poured it out onto the ground near them, which brought on some unhappy muttering. She was afraid of what could happen to them around the machinery, etc. I believe my mother really hated the "demon rum".

It took many men and boys to do these chores. A farmer most likely owned his tractor, plows, rakes, etc., but big machinery was borrowed or rental machinery was brought out from town for many of them. Dad let me hand out the small amount of money--always cash--to pay the hired men, some years just one dollar a day.

After the men ate their noon meal (more like a feast what with Mama's cooking and the food brought in by women in the neighborhood to help out), they rested under the trees in the front yard for a short spell and riled up Jake and me into a wrestling match (thank goodness for bloomers). I won for many years--I think they were laying bets--but it all stopped when Jake finally grew up some and whomped me and I became more grown up and ladylike, not so rough-and-tumble.

There were many lean years, caused mainly by drought, which meant dust storms and low yields, or too much rain which meant flooded fields, and sometimes by the swarms of different kinds of invading insects ravaging the crops in the fields.   Mostly I remember them as good years, because we always had food to eat and a place to live, even if the crops didn't "make" it.

Farmers in our part of the country didn't retire, except in a case of very serious illness or death when their children took over the running of the farms.   Sometimes a few acres were rented out to a family under the condition that they would farm the land or at least help with it. In Mama's case, when Dad died she was put into the government's soil conservation program covering some of her acreage. She was paid a yearly stipend for letting the land remain uncultivated and unplanted, which was a godsend for her.

SHARE THE WORK

Butchering time of pork and beef was something else neighbors shared. The men picked out the animals and did the main butchering and their wives helped cut the meat into whatever pieces they wanted. Cattle bought and fattened for butchering were not pinned up then; consequently, the meat probably would not pass present-day tenderness standards, but we did not know the difference.

The kids had the job of walking around and around the big, hot, black wrought iron kettle kept on the east side of the smokehouse, stirring the lard that was being rendered from the many pieces of fat and rind being cut off the pork meat. Chewing on the hot "cracklins" was a reward for circling that hot pot.

My family's share of the meat was taken into the smokehouse and covered with a brine mixture that preserved it for the long winter to come. I remember having trouble when I was very young bringing in the right cut of meat for my mother, no matter how many times she showed me. Pork ribs looked to me the same as a beef roast under all that salt. Round steaks were pounded (and pounded) with a square wooden or aluminum mallet with prongs for tenderizing. We did not have "hamburger" for many years. We had big meat grinders for making coarse sausage, seasoned and canned by the women.

Besides using the big black kettle outside to heat laundry water and render lard, sometimes the neighbor women used it to make lye soap, which was good for getting one clean after a day of chores, even if it did dry out the skin, and it helped with stains in the laundry. Mama also bought Lava bar soap. Milder soaps were bought or made for regular bathing and washing hair.

Our orchard was a favorite place, especially at canning time, when relatives and neighbors brought what they had of their own fruit and vegetables, and Mama shared some of ours. Canning meat, fruits and vegetables was a long tedious job including scalding Mason jars and lids and sealing them tightly. Some used pressure cookers.

Apples ran a good chance of having a worm and some rot, but a quick knife cut could take care of that. We had pear trees and peach trees in the orchard. Insecticides were not sprayed on anything, so we were free to eat straight from the bushes or orchard trees, dust and all, but they were washed for cooking and canning. We had grapevines and a large blackberry patch at the western edge of the yard. I remember when that patch burned during one night; it was never known why, tho' there were many guesses.

Wild blackberries became a favorite must after the tame patch burned, and gooseberries were a must for many

of us, though it was a lot of trouble to pick and can
them. For protection we dressed in Dad's old, every-
day pants and shirts, wore hats, gloves and boots to
ward off mosquitoes, bees, gnats, etc. and spent several
hours in the woods and fencerows with our buckets,
trying to ignore thoughts of any lurking snakes. We
were pretty proud of the many berries we were able
to bring home for Mama to use. She canned lots of
them for making blackberry and gooseberry cobblers
to enjoy later in the year. Now, sometimes a small
branch is brought in for easier picking. Fran freezes
some berries; she says there are many bushes left in the
forests around their farm.

Neighbor women and relatives came to make and can
apple butter to enjoy during the coming winter. There
was a huge copper kettle (almost every farm woman
around borrowed this miracle kettle from Aunt Minnie)
in the middle of the fire in the side yard. The women
cleaned and cored apples and threw the pieces into the
big kettle along with sugar, ground cinnamon and oil
of cinnamon, a pinch of salt now and again. We young
girls took turns walking around the hot pot, stirring
continuously with a special big curved wooden paddle
provided.

Apple butter has always been one of my favorite foods,
but in all this time, I have never found any that tasted as
good as what they made then. Mama's pickled peaches
were eye-closing mmmmmm good and she was told
she made the best. Mama also made a lot of jam and
jelly; her tomato preserves were also favorites. Home-

canned vegetables and fruits got us through many a cold winter, stored in the cellars, which have their own smell.

There was the mulberry tree; Mama didn't can or preserve those berries, so we kids spent a lot of time draped on the limbs of that tree, and came out with purple lips and fingers from eating them. Many other things were not canned. Paw-paws were favorites of some, but not for me, and there were tart persimmons to pucker you up, but they were much better when fully ripe.

HOLIDAY & OTHER SPECIAL FUN

WE MADE LITTLE OF NEW Year's Day, but Valentine's Day was something special. We made our own valentines in school, and everybody got one from everybody else, including the teacher. The little, hard sugar-candy hearts with "messages" on them were something to wish for. Many adult valentine cards--found in our attic-- were works of art, some made with paper doilies and sometimes with real lace. They had pictures on them of beautiful ladies in fancy dresses and men dressed in fancy clothes, and had very flowery verses.

Easter was one of the most enjoyable holidays. The day before Easter, we were allowed to help color (dye) the eggs after they had been boiled, and we put them in a big basket on the dining room table....not to be eaten just yet. While we slept, the Easter Bunny hid all colors and sizes of hard candy eggs in the yard under bushes and in tall grass, behind trees, in rocky places, etc.; softer candies such as chocolate bunnies and eggs were hidden in the house, but not so well that they wouldn't be found right away.

Little straw baskets with ribbons were filled and delivered to close-by favorite or ill neighbors or relatives. Seems some things haven't changed much.

Summers were fun, especially on holidays. Memorial Day was a time for dressing up and visiting the nearby family cemeteries, remembering good and bad things, crying, and laughing at fun memories. Most of the years our home was the gathering place for kinfolks on this day as we didn't live far from the Fulton graveyard. The women picked fresh flowers from their own gardens and bushes for this day of decorating the graves--no grave was left without flowers.

Annabelle said she heard when she was a child (no confirmation) that when the Civil War ended, Great Grandpa Ira Thomas Fulton, a young man then, moved to the area from Fulton County, Arkansas, and bought many acres of farmland. His dad, also named Ira, came to visit him and died during that visit. They were unable to get him back to Arkansas for burial in those days, so buried him on the land there and started the Fulton Cemetery at that time. Many of the old tombstones are unreadable now due to spalling and crumbling.

On these Memorial Days, aunts, uncles and cousins of all ages gathered at our house and yard after, bringing in "covered dishes" of all kinds of good things to eat at the make-shift tables and benches set up in the yard by the men. The kids played games--tag, andy-over, darebase, kick the picket and anything else we could think of or had the energy for. Grownups visited, remembering, sometimes sadly and sometimes laughing loudly with their tears. Some years this was during the time of the extended visits from out-of-town kinfolks.

Later in the day we gathered more flowers and took them to the nearby Dodson Cemetery where Mama's relatives were buried, and spent some time there with Mama's small family.

About the same time, the Wills family (which included anyone, like us, who was kin in some way) had a huge family reunion in the big yard at the home of Herman and Dolly Wills. Their son, Charles Lee, a buddy of Jake and Wade, had thick blond curly hair. There, too, were big tables loaded with all kinds of food; games, gossip and laughter went on until chore-time. I heard recently that it is still being held on the second Sunday of June each year. I regret that the Fulton reunion is no longer held.

Many other times during the summer we picnicked and enjoyed wading in the numerous nearby shallow streams with gravel beds, no mud, and some cold deep pools of dark blue-green water under a canopy of leafy tall trees. There were deeper, fast-running rivers nearby, too, where people, mostly the men-folk, floated in rustic canoes or flat-bottomed boats in the smooth wide spots and enjoyed catching catfish, perch, etc. for our supper on nearby picnic tables. Kids enjoyed swimming around the permanent rafts there or playing tag, catch and other games in the adjacent shoreline parks.

Fourth-of -July was for many years the time for a big family picnic at the Finley River near Ozark. The main meat was fried chicken. Kids were not allowed to swim for 30 minutes after eating. We did such a good job of waiting that I don't remember even one kid with a case of stomach cramps, although the complaining and whining was enough to drive any listening parent crazy! I wonder today if it were true or an old wives' tale.

The river had a fifteen-feet-high dam with clear, cool water rushing over it. Most of the kids gleefully ran back and forth under the waterfall there, but it took me a little time to be brave enough for that and I had to hold my nose to do it. I still have a fear of bridges--especially modern-day high ones--and dams, lakes, or any large bodies of water.

At one of the picnics, our cousin Gwenny from Wisconsin was stung by a wasp. One of the jovial tobacco-chewing uncles stuck a big wad of his chewed tobacco on the sting and, like magic, she said it felt much better soon after. The fireworks were small and sparse--we weren't used to anything elaborate anyway-- but we had wonderful family fun!

Sometimes on the 4th of July we went to downtown Rogersville for a fair or carnival and fireworks. Grapette and Orangette were big treats, as was a vanilla, chocolate, or strawberry ice cream cone.

There was one big tent where tickets were sold to see a movie inside. I don't remember the price of admission, but it was usually sold out. My brothers and some of their friends joined other boys as they sneaked in under the edges of the tent after the lights were out and watched the shows, if they didn't get caught. With any luck at all, one might find a large enough hole in the side of the ragged, much-used tent to take a peak from the outside.

It was usually a cowboy movie--Tom Mix, Tex Ritter, Gene Autry, Wild Bill Hickock or such. Sometimes there wasn't a movie, but loud live country music with a few sparsely-clad girls jiggling about on stage; they gave a mild preview on a stage in front of the tent; kids were not allowed inside the tents to see those shows .

Besides the show tent, there were stalls for ring toss and other games, stalls where we could buy three softballs and throw them at bowling pins or a moving target of some kind and, if we were lucky, win a handsome rag or sock doll or stuffed animal. At other stalls, we could take a chance on winning a prize by hitting a small target with a softball and dropping a young man (usually a local high school boy) into a tank of water. In Rogersville and other small towns around everyone played softball, so the young man took a bath every few minutes! Some stalls awarded Kewpie dolls to winners. There were also numerous other games of skill there.

When it was a fair, women from all around the area brought their home-made quilts, embroidered tea towels and pillow cases, baby clothes and crib furnishings, etc., home-cooked and home-canned items, many cakes and pies to be judged. There were special horses, cattle, calves, pigs, sheep, poultry, etc. brought in to be judged, many of them by proud high school kids.

Halloween was not as big a deal then as now. We did not dress up in costume and call on neighbors or relatives for candy or other treats. Neighbors lived too far apart and transportation was just not there for such activities, even if we had thought of them. Older boys did do some things they thought were funny; their main enjoyment seemed to be moving the outdoor toilets to far away places or turning them over, and sometimes they moved cars and trucks around from one farm to another. Their parents and neighbors failed to see any humor in these cute tricks. We also never had our house tee-peed--there was no toilet paper!

Thanksgiving was spent with family at someone's home; roast chicken, or chicken and dumplings or noodles was the main meal on that day when we were younger, but later Mama did raise a few turkeys. That was one of the times we went down into the cellar and brought out goodies stored there from the summer's (hopefully) bountiful crops, tasty reminders and payoffs of some of Mama's hard summer work.

Christmastime meant homemade decorations, tinsel, etc.; we did not have a tree inside our home. We didn't think it strange that there was no fireplace "chimbley" for Santa to come down. Christmas also meant hanging our longest brown stockings on doorknobs or on nails, real stockings decorated with cutouts or crayon drawings of Santa Claus, reindeer, etc. We looked for the largest stockings we could find and took the same place each year to hang them. I remember the excitement, fitful sleep, the waiting for morning to come.

Many toys had to be placed under the stockings because of size. Stockings were filled with wrapped hard candy, small toys such as jacks, balls, and real live oranges! Wherever in the wide world did Santa find real live oranges in the cold of winter? We also sometimes received a coloring book or a book of paper dolls and most times there were new little iron toy tractors or trucks. Anyway, many of the toys could and would be shared. Whatever we received was not wrapped in beautiful paper and ribbons, and there were no beautiful gift tags or cards.

We each received only one special toy; we were told that Santa had too many stops to make and children to please for any one of us to receive more than our share. One year I received a 10" tall Shirley Temple doll and knew it to be the most beautiful thing in the world! No sharing that!

Christmastime also meant a party at the grade school. There were decorations at all the windows, all made by the students. There were skits by the students, given for the parents and anyone else who wanted to be there. There was always the prayer by a preacher. Parents brought plenty of food; we sang Christmas carols and there was wonderful fellowship. At first, nobody thought anything at all about the tall pine tree that had been cut down one year and brought in, decorated with tinsel, paper loops, and a few real, BURNING CANDLES in special holders! THAT didn't happen again!

There were pie suppers at the schoolhouse, too. Each girl and woman brought either a box of homemade candy, a pie, cookies or a cake, covered with a tea towel, napkin or other cloth so as to be a surprise to the buyer. The boys and the men held a bidding war for the items, not knowing who brought what, and ate with the one who "brung" it. The money they raised--it seemed like a lot then--went for things the school needed. The most important thing was the fun and fellowship. Some of the men brought out their fiddles and livened things up a lot. There was no dancing allowed at schools then, but kids were allowed to "jig" a little bit. Yes, there was time for prayers there, too.

There were shivarees for newly married couples. The time of the shivaree was not announced to the young couple. They knew to expect it, but didn't know how long after the wedding it would be until they would be awakened in the wee hours of the morning by loud yelling and off-key singing, accompanied by beautiful music played on pots, pans and washboards with sticks or metal utensils, and any other lovely music that could be imagined, along with the horn honking of the assembled cars and pickups.   Any real musical instrument only accidentally ever hit a true note at the exact right moment!

Young just-married couples kept clothes handy for hasty donning until the "event" was over. They were loudly requested to light lamps or lanterns and come outside with their smiling faces and greetings and maybe pass out some cookies or peanut butter crackers they had prepared for this welcoming event. There was much laughter and joking, and much well-wishing for the new couple.

There were many other occasions where neighbors got together to celebrate something or just have some fun-- this in addition to days spent in sympathy for neighbors and relatives in times of trouble or heartbreak.

GRADE SCHOOL

I SAT ON OUR DECK IN a shady spot; it was a warm, lazy day. Several cars drove by. Some young kids on bikes rode by, laughing and talking, on their way home from a nearby grade school. Those kids made me think again with mixed emotions of my younger days, school days, days that began my merging shyly into a larger society.

Wolf Grade School on Wolf Trail was a small local one-room school building painted white. It had a big black wood-burning furnace used for heating the building during the cold, bleak southern Missouri winters when an angry wind howled outside, nothing to stop it. There was a cloakroom/closet with room also for storage of sports equipment, etc. Two sturdy wooden two-hole toilets called "outhouses", one for girls and one for boys, were located way out at the edge of the school property near the ball diamond--wonderful for winter days!

During my earliest years, we took our own lunches in little rectangular black tin lunchboxes; most of the time lunch was peanut butter or mashed pinto beans on a biscuit; it sometimes included some raisins and/or an apple or peach in season. There was no refrigeration, so we couldn't take meat or eggs except on frigid days to be kept outside. If

I didn't want or like my lunch, I told Mama that Cletus DeWitt took it--I don't think he ever knew he was a thief!

There was but one teacher for all eight grades (no kindergarten there); there weren't many students in each grade, and many of them were related--cousins, as well as brothers and sisters. All told, there was an average of between thirty-five to fifty students during each of those years. Most of them had walked or ridden their bikes to school.

Starting from the left side of the open room, facing the teacher and the blackboard behind her on the north wall were individual and some double wooden slant-top desks with the seats attached, for the youngest children. Moving to the right, individual desk sizes increased, most of them knife-scarred in some way by initials, hearts, etc.; all had narrow grooves on top for pencils and small drawers for supplies.

Each school day a couple of the older boys "ran up" the American flag on a pole just outside the front door, and they carefully took it down at the end of the day. We lined up and said the Pledge of Allegiance with our hands held over our hearts; we did as well as we could in singing the national anthem; I think each of us had our own version of it. The day was started with the Lord's Prayer and the younger ones had their own version of that.

We brought from home our lead pencils, big pink rubber erasers (used a lot), crayons, Big Chief lined tablets and 3-ring binders complete with paper that we had helped our mothers buy at our small nearby store in Mentor. We had ink pens that we dipped into a small bottle of black ink, then again as needed. We vigorously practiced our push-pulls and ovals in penmanship class, and always took home some kind of homework to be done by ourselves as much as possible. There were no large reference libraries around us, but dictionaries and World Books were available at school and we were obliged and encouraged to use them.

I never did figure out that giving a "kurnyven" was really a "current event" assignment, but I never missed having one. I knew I was to get them from the newspaper but never made a connection because of the hillbilly sound of those words, I guess.

I remember one very young early-grader who, while reciting in a bashful stammer in front of the whole school her assigned lesson, started at the hem of her dress and rolled up her skirt in a tight little roll; when she reached the point near the waistline, she very slowly rolled it back down. After her story was finished, she RAN back to her seat. Who knows what she said? Boys, especially, didn't stand straight and tall while reciting their assignments or stories; they shoved their hands into the pockets of their overalls, scratched themselves, fidgeted from foot to foot and twisted their bodies around in several contortions. Who knows what they said????

Some of our teachers were so-so; one or two were excellent. I was lucky to have one of the excellent ones, Mr. Ralph Martin, knowledgeable in all subjects, for the last three of my grade-school years. We had a new student one year who talked out loud constantly to "Mawten", wouldn't stay in his seat, walked right up at any time to Mr. Martin's desk and leaned against him, tried to sit on his lap, and disrupted the whole school. After some time spent working with him during and after regular school hours, "Mawten" had him calmed down somewhat. Teachers were not particularly pleased when some of the boys all held up their hands at once and snapped their fingers repeatedly to be called on for an answer (most often purposely wrong) to the teacher's question. Neither did they like the many paper "airplanes" nor the sling-shot paper wads flying around the room. I've noticed over the years that none of my boy classmates has been President, Senator, a judge or a teacher! Seriously, they did turn out fine in the long run, respectful, respected and loved.

There was a Miss Bea Hall, who was a great teacher of spelling, grammar, etc. She helped make a state spelling champion of my sister Fran. Our cousin Dorothy Fulton taught there for a few years, after I was gone; Wade got several of his many spankings from her for his non-stop talking and making the others laugh.

New teachers and the few substitute teachers we often had were in for some fun--I'm sure they knew from earlier experiences and gossip what was coming. All of the boys answered roll call to the wrong names, answering for someone else (a game seemingly passed down to each new first grade boy) and the rest of us weren't to laugh. It usually took a few days for those patient teachers to get straight all the faces and the names that went with them.

Music was mostly learned at home, if one were lucky enough to have parents or relatives who had any knowledge at all of any instrument. In all probability, the instrument would be a piano or a fiddle. Sometimes a music teacher would come to our school just to teach us scales, time and notes, and the names of musical instruments--hard to remember if you are not around them some. We did sing--mostly hymns, rounds and the favorites of that time and place, country music. Annabelle had a piano that I tried and tried to play, but, with no teacher, it was mostly noise. How in the world did she stand that racket? She was, and still is, a dear cousin and a great friend.

We chose up sides for spelling bees, ciphering (arithmetic) matches and geography contests, all of which I thought I should win. For fun, we learned that one way to remember how to spell geography was by saying "George Everett's Oldest Girl Rode A Pig Home Yesterday". To remember how many days are in each month, we made a fist and, starting with an outside knuckle, named the months; knuckles' months have 31 days, "valley" spaces have 30 days, or in the case of February, 28 or 29.

There were no organized exercise or gym classes, no calisthenics; we didn't need them--we were constantly very active. We had great games chasing each other in the deep snows that fell on the schoolyard. In nice weather we had gunnysack races and there was the three-legged race where your partner's leg was tied to yours as you ran toward a finish line. There were no field trips to the zoo or to an aviary in our earliest years.

There were no birthday parties. We received homemade birthday cards from our schoolmates, made at school; some were more artistic and interesting than others, but that made no difference to us.

In grade school and into high school there were no Boy Scouts or Girl Scouts in our part of the country; we weren't out selling Girl Scout cookies. We were introduced to 4-H clubs and to the Future Farmers of America. They impressed upon us the importance of responsibility and respect for other people, the land, and the animals thereon. The boys learned about farm things. In conjunction with what our mothers taught us, we girls became more knowledgeable about cooking, sewing, running a home, decorating, gardening, etc. The 4-H pledge was:

> **"I pledge my head to clearer thinking,**
> **my heart to better loving,**
> **my hands to greater service**
> **and my health to cleaner living"**

and our song was:

> **"I know a place where the sun is like gold,**
> **and the clouds are as white as snow,**
> **and down underneath is the loveliest**
> **place, where the four-leaf clovers grow.**
> **One leaf is for hope, and one is for**
> **faith, and one is for love, you know.**
> **And God put another one in for luck.**
> **If you search, you will find where they grow.**
> **But you must have hope, and you must have faith,**
> **you must love and be strong, and so,**
> **if you watch, if you wait,**
> **you will find the place**
> **where the 4-leaf clovers grow."**

Our sports equipment was not much; we had several softballs and bats, stuffed canvas bases, some softball gloves (mitts)--all of this soon became pretty well-worn. Most of the boys had their own gloves--Christmas presents, probably. We had a few basketballs and indoor games such as dominoes and checkers. Competitive sports were important to all the families of little country schools and expanded our realm of friends.

I was in the second grade and was initiated into the rabid softball "club" when I happened to be far out in the "field" in a game of "scrub". A tall fly ball fell into my outstretched skirt. Most of the kids laughed, but the older boys didn't think it was too funny. I was rewarded with a turn at bat, but that wasn't anything to brag about nor to worry those boys and lasted only through three strikes. I knew absolutely nothing about any of it.

It did spark my interest, though, and I began trying to learn the game. "Scrub" was the game played most of the time because of the various ages, sizes and knowledge of the game of the kids available. We had many opportunities to learn all positions as everyone moved up a notch as each out was made--shortstop to third base to second base to first base, etc. One day when I had finally moved up to be the catcher, the boy pitching was older and pretty good; the batter missed the ball, which hit me smack in the middle of my nose--it was not broken, luckily! My two swollen black eyes lasted a few days. I was determined to learn, though, and now professional baseball is a favorite with me.

When I was older and smarter about the game, Wolf grade school had a championship boy/girl team at the Rally (Field)

Day in the big town of Springfield; I was the first baseman. We won! We couldn't believe we won! The boys' team we beat was really MAD because they had been beaten by a small-school team with "girls"!

One of our favorite yells was: "Pitcher's sick and throwing up", which we thought might somehow throw off an opposing pitcher. And we were told repeatedly to hold the brand up when batting, so the bat wouldn't split.

A district school nurse was sent out monthly to rural schools. She taught us about sanitation, how to brush our teeth correctly, she checked us for unhealed injuries and left us some bandages and minor medicines. She checked each of us for head lice and advised our parents what to do about them if found. My family didn't have them. She was there for any outbreak of croup, diphtheria or pneumonia, and any other contagious threat such as measles and mumps.

One day Mama took me to Woolworth's dime store in Springfield to buy my first bra. I was embarrassed to death! The underwear counter was smack in the middle of the store, and anyone around (I imagined there were thousands of people there) could see Mama trying the bras on me over my dress. I took good care of that bra so that I wouldn't have to go through that any more!

Mama hadn't told me ahead of time about girls' periods. I was almost thirteen and at the grade school when I felt a little twinge of dizziness and there was blood. I thought maybe I was dying, but from what? The teacher let me lie down for a little while then sent me to the nearest neighbor. That poor woman knew just what to do; she had been through this experience many times. She was very gentle with me and fixed me up but left it to my mother to tell me about it, and at least reassured me that I was perfectly healthy.

Mama tore up old, clean sheets (sheets--how many sheets could she have had?) and tea towels, folded them for pads and made a wide elastic belt to hold everything in place with big diaper pins. Mama did tell the other two girls what to expect. I made sure my own daughter knew years ahead of time. I was backing out of the drive heading for work when I saw her leaning against the garage door, head drooping, lips pouting, looking out from under lowered eyelids. I got out, hugged her, fixed her up with better resources than I had had many years before, and reassured her; after that first day she informed me it went fine but she wasn't going to do it again!

Trouble was, why didn't someone tell the boys about it? What were they to think? There was much whispering and some snickering among them when the lines of the belt, etc. showed under the girls' dresses or when the girls felt a little under the weather and didn't make a good showing in sports events that day. It was very embarrassing for the girls. I, as well as my daughter later, had terrible cramping, as did many of our friends. If men can put a man on the moon, why can't they fix this universal problem? If they had to go through it, I'm sure they would help come up with some way to relieve it immediately and forever!

All things considered, grade school years were lots of fun and I loved the learning part.

SPECIAL NEW THINGS

THE NEXT SUMMER DAY AFTER the concrete was poured for the new two-lane U.S. Highway 60 two miles away to the north of us, many neighbors came to see it finished and cleaned up. This highway was very important to them for their farming activities.

When the workers left after their clean-up, the kids (most of us barefoot) took to that warm new smooth pavement and ran each direction, back and forth, as fast as we could run; it was late in the afternoon and, because the concrete was curing, we never saw a single car that day, although we had been firmly warned by our parents to be careful of everything.

The highway ran up and down the many hills and around the many curves--unlike the wide, straight, level highways of today--all the way to town to the west and way out who knew where to the east. Each farmer along the way had to provide his own driveway onto it, preferably at the top of a rise in the pavement. There were many of them and they had to be very careful when entering the highway with trucks and machinery; they caught onto driving uphill on the dirt shoulders for safety's sake.

Woe to any stray animals that couldn't be seen over the hills of the road--hard on vehicles, too!

The WPA (Works Progress Administration) workers put in a good gravel road in front of our home; that was the Greene/Christian county line and it was pretty busy for a country road. The workmen had their packed lunches, but Mama gave them water and sometimes homemade cookies or cake. The dust they stirred up was something awful. Road graders were driven on the new road somewhat regularly afterward, following a big water-dispensing truck, to try to keep it smooth. So many rocks! Good luck!

As a very young girl, I visited several times with a friend who lived in Springfield. I watched in admiration and wonder as she carried around the living room a black hand-held telephone with a long cord, sometimes lying on the floor or on the sofa with her feet thrown up on the back of it. She laughed and talked so comfortably, confidently and casually; I would have been so self-conscious and tongue-tied.

Not long after that our telephone line was installed, which in rural areas was a party line, and every farmer had his own "ring". Our telephone was a big, tall walnut box that hung on the hall wall; it had a crank on its right side that was used to do the rings--longs and shorts; our ring was two longs and a short. We spoke into a round metal mouthpiece on the front. We kids were advised not to use it unless necessary. It was pretty well known that neighbors not only received their own calls but also listened in on--and even joined--calls to others. "Party" line was a good name for it.

I stayed overnight in the beautiful new home of another city friend and was fascinated on Sunday morning by the sun's shining brightly through a big "picture" window in the cozy living room. That bright warm sunlight fell upon the pages of the Sunday Springfield News and Leader which were lying scattered about on a colorful sun-drenched rug.

In the center of their front lawn they had a large woven-wood arbor painted white that was covered with blooming red roses and ivy. I thought it to be lovely.

We had a small battery-powered radio we listened to, static and all, as it faded in and out constantly. Radios were improved from time to time and we were always happy to get a newer one. There were no remote controls; we had to go to the radio to change or tune in manually the few stations.

Everything stopped for Dad's news programs. We all gathered around to listen to the good comedy shows--Jack Benny, Henry Aldrich, Gildersleeve, Burns and Allen were very funny shows. None of us wanted to miss the scary shows like Innersanctum, The Shadow Knows, etc.

When I was about fourteen, I taught myself to dance by myself in the parlor to the music coming from the radio. Music made the ironing go by a little faster, too.

When we were young children, there were no newspapers delivered to the farms; sometimes Dad would bring one from town. In that newspaper, we became acquainted with the Katzenjammer Kids, Li'l Abner, Popeye, Gasoline Alley, and Little Henry, who could do very little right (we many times called Wade "Little Henry").

Dad was a sports fan, and kept up with the St. Louis Cardinals' baseball team, especially. Once in a while there would be a McCalls or Ladies Home Journal magazine lying around, probably one received from someone who had already read it. They presented to us a mighty different world from our own.

We kids, though, enjoyed the Sears, Roebuck catalog more than anything. We read and reread it; it truly was a "wish book" full of riches we could hardly imagine. The clothes and accessories, the furniture and house wares didn't interest us for very long but any kind of advertising for cars was devoured. I wish now that we had saved a catalog for later years to enjoy seeing the way things were made to be better, but had no idea how styles, inventions, etc. would change our lives.

Old catalogs and any newspapers were used in the outhouse.

THE BIG TOWN

IT DIDN'T TAKE LONG TO put away the few things I bought at the nearby Jones department store this day. Neither John nor I really needed much of anything, certainly not clothes, although I, as so many women do, enjoy just browsing around in almost every department. There is some satisfaction in having enough dishes and linens so as not to worry about it; we are not heavy entertainers now and don't need any additional fancy things. It would have been nice for Mama to have had more pretty selections and the means to take advantage of them. One good thing we kids did for her enjoyment: We all chipped in later and bought her a TV.

Downtown Springfield had a square, as did most of the towns back then, especially county seats. There was a big round "pie" in the middle with a concrete walkway crisscrossing it, a few park benches, trees, grass and some flower beds. Signs at this pie directed traffic to circle it to the right and there were no stop signs or lights there. It led to Boonville Street to the north, where the Court House was located, St. Louis Street to the east, South Street to the south, and City Highway 66 to the west. There were many lovely churches representing different denominations scattered throughout Springfield, each had its own beautiful tall spire, different from the others, reaching high into the sky.

As children, we thought Springfield to be huge and a quite wonderful place to visit, even for just a drive through it. Many people sat on the lawn or on the benches inside the circle park and watched as other people drove by or walked along the streets, calling out greetings to those they knew passing by. It was a very special place to be at Christmastime with all its decorated store windows and light poles, bells ringing, etc.

Heers Department Store was on the northwest corner of the square; Barb worked there for a while. Landers Department Store was on the west side and so was Newberry's; W. T. Grant was on one corner of South Street. The J. C. Penney Company store was next to the Fox Theater on the north corner at the east side. The Fox Theater showed regular first-line movies. Kresge's, which many years later became a K-Mart, was on the south side, east of the Mozark Theater.

The Mozark for many years showed mostly Westerns-- "cowboy" movies. Besides the weekly scary serials, there were movies with Gene Autry (who went into the service during World War II), Tom Mix, the Lone Ranger, Red Rider, Roy Rogers and Dale Evans, Ken Maynard and others who were popular at the time. This theater was where my cousin Hazel took me to see my first Shirley Temple movie. I absolutely adored her! I HAD to have the Shirley Temple doll after that! I still think she was one of the cutest kids I've ever seen.

These movie houses and the radio were our parents' means of staying up with the news on all fronts. We were not old enough to be aware of Prohibition days and of the gangsters such as Pretty Boy Floyd, Baby Face Nelson, Bonnie and Clyde, John Dillinger, etc. We were sheltered from all that although the names came up.

Sears, Roebuck & Co. was on Campbell Street, where most of the bars and poolhalls (almost all on the second floors) were located. Women were not welcome in those places. The Shrine building was located close to the Fox Theater; the Masonic Hall was a few blocks away. There were libraries, many cafes and other stores on nearby streets, and many manufacturers, canneries and dairies, car and heavy equipment dealers, etc. in town; there were very few specialty stores.

We often went by bus on class trips to the roller skating rink in town, spending a lot of time on the floor there, and occasionally went to the zoo on an all-school trip. There were several public parks in the city, some with swimming pools and ball diamonds, etc., all heavily used.

It wasn't until I had graduated from high school and moved there to work that I really became acquainted with the city of Springfield. It had spread out and grown so much by the time I went to Southwest Missouri State Teachers College there in the fall. It really changed and expanded quickly during and after the war was over and grew into the central place to be for many businesses and for cultural and community events.

It became an important hub for people from the many little towns and farms located around it. It soon was considered to be a gateway to the developing tourist centers to the south such as Rockaway Beach, Branson and Silver Dollar City.

HIGH STYLE

MEN AND WOMEN WORE HATS most of the time. Dad wore dark felt hats in the wintertime; they looked exactly like those worn by all the other men. At least the dress-up hats worn by the women had a little variety in the ribbons, feathers, etc., although farm women wore stiff-billed bonnets or straw hats for chores out in the sun.

Dad always had a farmer's straw hat for farm work and it had to be replaced often because of the effects of sweat, dust, rain, etc. Dad had heavy work gloves; I don't recall that Mama had any gloves except for dress--white rayon or cotton in summertime and black in wintertime.

When did Mama find time to do all the sewing she did, along with cooking, gardening, cleaning, laundry, etc.? My sisters and I always had enough dresses, matching bloomers, etc. for both grade school and everyday wear--no shorts, slacks, jeans, etc. then. Many were hand-me-downs from me to Barb to Fran. Mama most often used patterned flour sacks (mostly florals, checks, plaids or stripes in pastel and muted colors) for our dresses, and only occasionally a pretty muslin or percale print fabric from the store. She also sometimes had the fabrics Dad brought home from his trips. It was the same for the boys' shirts and undershorts.

She had just one pair of scissors that she was constantly losing (I'm sure the kids had a hand in that) and she was always begging for someone to find them for her. She also had one aluminum thimble with a small, pretty flower design painted on it. She used it constantly for sewing, embroidery work, mending and quilting, and, as far as I know, she never lost it!

Because Mama lost her one pair of scissors a hundred times a day and we were always looking for them and for her glasses (which usually had food splattered all over them), I go overboard and keep a scissors of some size in every room--meat cutters, paper cutters, one for thinning and one for cutting hair, nails, an old pair for trimming small plants and a couple of extras just in case--and I keep two pairs of glasses and many hair brushes handy.

She measured the yard goods she did buy by holding one end of the fabric to the tip of her nose and holding the length of the fabric along her outstretched arm, which was considered to be roughly a yard. The dresses she made for our everyday use were a little plainer than those she made for school or dress-up, which she fancied up with shirring, gathering, ric rac, bias tape, self-ruffles, sometimes lace and/or many colorful buttons, and many times they had a contrasting fabric yoke. Every dress had hand-sewn hems--short hems in ends of sleeves, wider, prettier hems in skirts.

She used Simplicity and McCalls packaged patterns, if any, and many times she mixed the two. Sometimes she laid a dress she liked directly upon the fabric on the big round oak table, worked it around and cut out the new dress from that. Some dresses hung from the shoulders and had either no belts or self-belts; sometimes there was a waistline and as many times not. They looked like originals no matter how she fashioned them or the decorations she used.

Skirts for me just barely reached the tops of the knees, whether straight or gathered; those for Barb and Fran were a little shorter; sleeves were usually puffed and collars (almost all dresses then had collars) were most often round Peter Pan style. The dirndl and Poodle skirts were popular a little later.

Garments buttoned either in the front or the back, buttonholes having been handmade by Mama. Her old Singer treadle sewing machine did not have a buttonhole attachment. There were no stretchy fabrics or zippers then. Bloomers had elastic in the waistline and it was used also to make gathered ruffles at the legs, both for "pretty" and privacy.

When I was a little older, I had a pair of black patent leather Mary Jane shoes to wear with my white cotton anklets, neatly turned down, for special occasions during the summer. In the wintertime, girls wore long, heavy, brown cotton stockings to the tops of the legs, with homemade elastic garters, and long-sleeved undershirts under their dresses which had been made of warmer fabrics. Long cotton underwear was a staple for Dad and the boys, too.

We had sturdy, high-top, black or dark brown shoes, black rubber galoshes, and warm woolen mittens in different colors, many times home-knitted by an aunt. Mama didn't knit.

There were no handy iron-on patches for mending tears and holes. Mama had to sew patches on by hand or machine. She always kept scraps for such use from the clothes she made us. Dad had a small triangle tear in one of his work shirts for many years. It was never mended and he had a small triangle of sunburn all summer on the back of his shoulder from wearing that shirt again and again every year. It became a family inside joke.

We didn't know what good "jewelry" was. Mama had no fancy rings, pins, necklaces, etc.; her wedding ring was a plain gold band. She had necklaces of some kind of beads or fake pearls, and she didn't wear earrings until much later. For my graduation from high school, my folks surprised me with a gold-toned Wittnaur watch. I thought it was the most beautiful thing I'd ever seen and wore it with pride for many, many years..

We started the new school year with new shoes. Last year's school shoes became every-day shoes if there was anything left of them after the real beating they had taken. Our shoes didn't have much style. They were either brown or black high-tops or oxfords. There were no thongs, high heels, sandals, or "tennis shoes".

I thought my feet were way too big and I tried repeatedly (unsuccessfully) to hide them under me whenever possible. When I was about nine I told Mama the new shoes--brown oxfords--were fine when we bought them at the store. It was raining; the drive home from town took a while. When I got out of the pickup and hit the ground, both of my feet were asleep and stinging and I bounced all the way into the house over that wet concrete sidewalk. I was extremely glad to mind my mother's orders to remove the shoes until schooltime the next day, which I now dreaded!

It took a long time to get them stretched out (more likely, worn out) so they were comfortable. I never did tell Mama and I never did that again. Even I knew that pride had to stop somewhere and this was it!

Another time, I hid my old shoes in the big sack of potatoes in the pantry and claimed they were lost so that I could wear the new shoes at once. I LIED! Mama found them soon when she went for potatoes to fix for dinner. I don't remember how she admonished me.

When we broke the shoestrings, we tied knots in them and restrung them through the eyelets. Our shoes were eventually very run down, mostly on the insides of the heels, so that Dad had to nail onto the soles small metal plates made for that purpose. There was not too much that could be done to "quick fix" the holes in the soles except to put some cardboard or cloth or both in the inside of the shoe or put on a glue-on sole until they could be resoled in town or we could get new shoes.

Not wearing shoes very often in the summertime helped cut down on that expense, anyway, although it widened our feet a bit.

Holes in our socks didn't always mean new socks; they were darned with matching yarn, by Mama on a darning egg or the bottom of a glass, and made a nice big uncomfortable blob in the toes and/or heels of our shoes.

Mama had long over-the-knee rayon hose held up with homemade elastic garters for "Sunday" wear, not many color choices; nylon hose weren't available to us until after the war. Eventually, I grew into store-bought cotton or rayon panties and a rayon slip and felt oh-so-grownup. Higher heels came much later.

Up until high school days, we didn't carry little purses as girls do now; a small sturdy brown sack was good enough for our lunches, or we took our lunches in little black metal boxes; some had thermoses. Girls did not carry combs, brushes, make-up, billfolds or change, etc., and we could stick a handkerchief in a pocket. Keys certainly weren't needed. Boys also had little need to tote around pocket change, combs, etc. but did carry a handkerchief in a pocket. We kept a small comb in our desks for when we came in from the wind, rain, etc.

HIGH SCHOOL HIGHS

Growing up has to be done. I did make it to high school. I was terribly shy on the big yellow bus that rumbled over the dusty country roads to pick us up and take us to the high school in Rogersville, in Webster County. The older kids seemed so much wiser, so casual and at ease. They didn't really tease us younger ones too much because they enjoyed the teasing with each other. I wondered if I would ever be so self-confident, but I did make some true friendships in high school. Not everyone was "kin" to me there!

The bus ride was about forty-five minutes long from our house because of the many pick-up stops.

Before the school year was halfway over, I had gained some self-respect and could join in the fun, but never was the initiator. I should have kept quiet. One of my most embarrassing moments was when I inadvertently blurted out for them to "look at that hop rabbit jacking off across the field". I didn't know until much later why the boys laughed so hard. One of the "boys" reminded me of this at a funeral down home recently!!

Having come from that little one-room white-painted wooden schoolhouse, I was very impressed with the big two-story red brick building that was my high school in

Rogersville. I remember when for some reason, early in my freshman year, I was alone outside the building on a balmy, beautiful sunshiny day, looked up and stood still just marveling at its beauty. I loved its many rooms, halls, wide wooden stairs and big windows.

I moved to stand with my back against its warm bricks and stretched out my arms as far as I could reach across them with my fingers spread wide apart, caressing their rough surfaces. I looked across its softball diamonds, oval outdoor track, tennis courts, and outside basketball goals, then up at the many windows. I felt so very lucky to be there and felt my warm tears on my cheeks. I loved being in the classrooms with so many other students, most of whom I had only recently met and many of whom would be my teammates in sports events, etc. I had so many teachers now, one for each subject, and there were so many books! This was a new world for me. I was so happy!

I was caught gossiping in the girls' dressing room in the high school gymnasium. It wasn't anything really bad, and I was mostly listening to the girls doing the talking, a big no-no. The girl being talked about opened a stall door and came out right into the middle of our group, looking both hurt and defiant. Silence! I felt so bad; I was speechless. It did teach me a lesson, though, and I decided to give up gossiping right then and there. I learned very quickly how it could unnessarily hurt someone and certainly not do me any good.........I'm afraid that I have slipped a few times.

I really admired and liked Mr. Riley, our school superintendent. He had very smooth tanned skin and was very tall and slim with coal black straight hair and almost black eyes, and I never saw him in anything but a black suit, white shirt, and a tie, spotlessly neat. I never knew if he were married and had kids.

He was also the citizenship class teacher and had a very dry sense of humor. He many times sat with his long legs stretched out and crossed at the ankles in front of him with his long feet in his shiny black shoes resting on his desk. His class was an easy one for me but one day I completely froze--a total blank--when he called on me to answer a question. He very kindly went to someone else and asked me later if I was o.k. I never figured out what happened, but it didn't happen again.

Miss Flett, a pretty, dark-haired little woman who was our shorthand and algebra teacher, told me right off the button in front of the whole new class that I would never amount to much! I never knew why she picked on me. I think in retrospect now that it was a dare, as I decided immediately to show her! She was always very nice and helpful to me after that day and called on me to help her when an occasion arose in class.

We had manual Royal typewriters and tried for a top speed of at least 60 words per minute, which included throwing the carriage back at the end of each line and for every paragraph. We ran copies off on a Ditto machine, which had purple ink. I still use shorthand on many occasions, having improved immensely after attending Chillicothe Business College. I used my knowledge of double-entry bookkeeping for many years after graduation working for companies long, long before they became computerized.

TVs, cell phones and computers were not even in our imagination yet.

Miss Flett's "boyfriend", Mr. Ashley, was our athletic coach, a very good one, a very easy-going, sandy-haired handsome man who dressed in varying colors of brown and tan. I never heard anything about their getting married or not. Mr. Ralph Hamilton took over for Mr. Riley when he retired. Mr. Hamilton turned 90 on June 28, 2006, according to a local Springfield paper. There were, of course, other fine teachers whose names escape me now, although I am very thankful for their time and effort on my behalf.

High schools then didn't have the discipline problems faced by faculty now. Any pupil sent to the principal's office was sorely ashamed and hoped it wouldn't get back to the parents. Discipline that started at home carried over from the lower grades into high school and consequently into later life. Teachers had the right to punish students for misdeeds. I never witnessed any over-zealousness; students sometimes had to leave the classroom, were awarded extra homework, or had to write over and over "I will never ....again".

Things were not as fast-paced then as now; I was finally getting into algebra, literature, debate, some music and in my senior year I got to learn some Spanish, which I enjoyed but never mastered enough to impress anybody; it was easier to speak it than to make out what someone else was saying. History and geography lessons became more complicated and interesting. We still knew nothing of rockets, space ships, etc., of course. Symphonic music and great art did not impress me or many of my friends as we had never before been exposed to them in any form and not much here.

I was fortunate enough to be in several of our all-school or senior plays that were performed for our families and friends, or for anyone who wanted to come. It was easy for me to memorize my lines, and many times those of the others. That didn't bother me much.

What did bother me much were the bright red splotches that showed up in numerous places on my face, mostly on my cheeks but maybe on one cheek and on the other side on the chin or eyelid, when it was time to perform on that stage in front of so many people. I think I must have willed them there! There seemed to be no way I could rid myself of them; I was so self-conscious. They probably weren't visible to the audience, but I FELT they were. They very conveniently disappeared when the play was over. It was another time when I was uncomfortable being the center of attention.

Basketball games and tournaments were big events in our part of the country for parents, other kin, friends and neighbors of all ages, all fiercely loyal to their favorite and local teams. They filled the fold-down metal chairs and wooden bleachers to overflowing in the hot, smelly, crowded gymnasiums where physical education (phys ed) classes and other games and events had been held that same day and many days, weeks and years before.

There was tension, constant loud, deafening yelling, accompanied and urged on by cheer leaders and some band instruments, prior to, during, and sometimes long after the end of the games; the teams played their hearts out after so many hours of practice. Emotions ran high and all involved were drained, players and spectators alike, at the end of the games, with heartbreak after a loss. These games were many times a small town's only claim to fame, and were a main topic of conversation all season long, with anticipation growing for the next game, even for the next year to begin.

We had excellent athletic teams. We rode busses to the "away games" schools where we would be competing; sometimes a few parents would be able to drive to the games. The girls played their volley ball games before the boys' basketball competition began. It was very loud on the busses, but not with cursing, dirty jokes or words; there was no fighting.

There was no time limit on taking basketball shots and scores were not as large as now. Our boys' basketball teams were champions of many tournaments while I was in high school; I almost fainted with excitement during their big games. It was fun being a cheerleader in our homemade, knee length, maroon pleated skirts and white sweaters with the big maroon "R" on the front. I was so hoarse after the games that I could barely talk. Our girls' volleyball and softball teams, too, were champions of our twelve-team league many years.

I learned to play competitive tennis and also enjoyed just volleying with my cousin Don Ferrell for many hours at a time after school hours.

I had no serious boyfriends; just fun friends with whom to go to a roller skating rink or to movies; we went on double dates or in groups that filled a car after I was sixteen. When we walked together on a sidewalk, the boys always walked on the outside, supposedly as protection for the girls - good manners left over from former times. There was no dancing in our high school either. Very few students went "steady" but many later romances and resulting marriages have lasted for a long time.

When I was a sophomore, I had my first real crush on the handsome, popular star of our basketball team, a senior, but he couldn't see me because of an "older woman" in his class. I did get to hold his sweat jacket sometimes during a game, between cheerleading duties.

One year our high school girls' softball team played tournament host to teams from several other schools, but failed to tell the diner and cafe owners in Rogersville about it. When we broke for lunch, they were overwhelmed with players and their orders. Several girls on our team immediately decided to forego our lunches and we helped them out, cooking, waiting tables, doing dishes, etc. I don't recall having ever seen such gratitude as they showed us that day; they offered free lunches to us, but time had run out. Going without lunch didn't seem to hurt us any; we won!

We girls worked very hard at being the best team around and became very good friends, visiting in each other's homes scattered throughout the area. One of my dear new friends was Ruby Smith. During my visit with her and her family one day, her father took us for a long ride in their new sedan. Before we left, he placed a large cord bag full of small Cokes in glass bottles in a niche between some rocks in the cold running water of a nearby stream for our enjoyment later; they were almost too cold to drink, sorta icy, but made a wonderful treat on that hot day.

Back then, girls were most likely to grow up to be teachers, secretaries, stenographers, clerks in a store or bank, or waitresses in a restaurant, unless they got married and had families and stayed home. We never knew of being flight attendants or nurses, and very few of us dreamed of going to live and work in larger cities. My brothers and their friends were destined to become farmers, truck or bus drivers, teachers, bookkeepers or maybe members of the Armed Forces. Several of my classmates were called into the armed services and were not present with us at our commencement exercises. World War II changed many things for lots of people.

Don Ferrel's family had the funeral home in Rogersville. Many times they called on one of our high school mixed quartets to sing at funerals. One particular funeral stands out in my memory. It was for an older woman, held at gravesite in a field near her home. In addition to the preacher, the gravediggers and our quartet, only her husband was there. The man's faded clothes were grimy, as were his hands. He was so sad, so alone. As we sang, a bee lit on Dean Palmer's nose; he crossed his eyes and watched it but didn't swat at it; it flew away shortly without causing any damage. Tears streamed down my face as we sang and my voice quivered. Was there no family? Were there no friends? Didn't anybody care?

This was so totally different from the time we sang at the funeral for one of our schoolmates where the church was packed to overflowing with family and friends. Everyone who could went to all funerals then and to the graveyards, after which they went to the home for awhile where women had brought in all kinds of food for those who were grieving and reminiscing.

World War II had been declared on December 8, 1941. My high school classmates that were called into military service were not present at our commencement in 1943. Several of those that had graduated before us were now in the armed services, too. For us, mostly, out in the country, time went on as usual; except for the servicemen, we seemed to be far removed from it, although Dad listened to the news reports on his small battery-run radio, whatever he could hear between the crackles and the static, and he got news from his friends when he went to the city.

I was in high school two years before Jake came; if he had listened, I would have taught him everything I knew about it! He was more interested in being on the basketball team and was a pretty darned good player. He was also good at holding the opponent's shorts by the hem so he couldn't move so quickly to the ball, a generally accepted form of fun for most of the players, I've heard. He was a very tall, slim kid then and took advantage of it.

I heard that Wade was good player, too, both basketball and softball, but I was gone by the time he made it to high school and outgrew the spankings. Both were strong as bulls due to their hard work on the farm. Barb, Weldon and Fran were all athletically inclined; I think Russ was, too.

Because I had excellent teachers and probably due to the books I had read in our attic, I was lucky enough to be valedictorian of my class--there were only forty-six of us; three of our boys went into military service in World War II. We always had a school "holiday" just before Commencement Sunday and our entire high school went to Fassnight Park in Springfield; we ate picnic lunches, sat in the shade of big trees, some rowed little boats in the lake; we were free to join in any games being played or just do whatever we wanted.

I had written out my valedictory address to study there, but had too much fun to do it and kept putting it off. I spent the day with my boyfriend Paul and many friends and getting my autograph book filled with witticisms of friends, some of whom I would never see again. I never did get the speech all memorized, and had to refer much too frequently to my notes, which embarrassed me to no end. I was so glad when it was ended and I quickly walked off the stage to what was polite applause, I think. It was totally unlike me to have done that but my shame didn't last too long.

Barb said the teachers were always throwing my name and grades up to them to try to get them all to do better. I received a one-year scholarship to Southwest Missouri State Teachers College in Springfield and a one-year scholarship to Chillicothe Business College, where I met John. I went to SMS after high school but didn't go to Chillicothe until after the war was over. Dad was gone then, so I was even more thankful for the scholarship they had given me. Mama had her hands full raising the younger ones.

SOUTHWEST MISSOURI
STATE TEACHERS COLLEGE

IN THE FALL, I TOOK advantage of my scholarship to Southwest Missouri State Teacher's College in Springfield. I found an apartment in a house near the college and Mama helped me make the clothes I would need; Dad gave me a little money for day-to-day expenses. I had never lived so close to an ice cream store before, and ate not much of anything else--mostly banana splits--for about two weeks! No telling how fat I would have gotten if I hadn't been so busy walking back and forth between buildings to all my classes, playing tennis, and taking phys ed courses.

I believe I would never have been able to go if it weren't for the scholarship. This was a big, new world for me. I did not know anybody. I was completely clueless about where I was to go to sign up for classes, and about where in the world these buildings were they had assigned me for classes. My biggest problem at first was finding my way around the campus! I finally got it figured out and also began to make some new friends, which was a big help. The number of students in each of my classes amazed me. This was NOT Rogersville High School!

There were young people from our state and from many nearby states and I began to meet some of them in our shared classes. I enrolled in a beginner's Spanish class, which I found fascinating but never mastered; I took a Bible class and enlarged in a small way my knowledge of that. I enrolled in Algebra, English and American History classes. My physical education (phys ed) class was swimming; I was determined by this time to learn how to swim and do so with confidence. I did become a little more proficient at it but didn't take the diving lessons. Going immediately with wet hair and damp clothes to another building for the next class was a bummer, especially in the fall and winter.

For the first time in my life, I was to experience the subtle differences between some of the moneyed coeds and those not so well-blessed. I began to see it in clothes, jewelry, makeup, poise, and sincerity (or lack thereof) of the spoken word. It became clear to me that I would never be invited to join the snootiest sororities, and, blessing of all blessings, I didn't care! I was never treated badly, just sometimes as if I weren't there and certainly by only a very few of them. I joined F-Square, a local sorority including farm and small-town girls like me, and we became good friends; there was no sorority house, no house mother, no competition for attention; we met in a schoolroom.

I began to hear about the college football team, "The Bears", and had no idea what they were talking about, when the season was cancelled because of the war.

There were Air Force Cadets on our campus; they were strikingly handsome and neat in their suntan uniforms and were so nice and so fun. It didn't take long to get acquainted with them. Many times I studied while sitting in the upper seats of the stadium, and I loved to watch them marching together and singing those little idiotic songs to stay in step. I had met many of them. One day they called to me to come down; they let me march in the right front and call a few moves, such as forward march, left face, right face, oblique and halt. It really was so much fun and I was so out of my element; that thoughtful out-of-the-ordinary act brought tears to my eyes and I will never forget it.

I started dating some of them occasionally, one of them more often than the others, a really polite, nice guy. Being naturally inquisitive, I asked a lot of questions about their life there; one evening he led me through the long, dimly lit, underground tunnel from the athletic field up to the entrance of their dorm to show me their quarters. The big room was also dimly lit and I could barely see them in their bunks and could hear them snoring (loudly) and was never so scared as I was at that moment at the thought of what would happen to me (and to him) if I were caught in that place! I turned and ran as fast as I could down and out of the tunnel until I was safely back in the stadium!

Freda McNeil moved in with me; I had worked with her in the pants factory the summer before and she was still working at the same place. She was a dark-haired, brown-eyed pretty girl with a wonderful smile and laugh, shorter than I, with a cute figure and a wonderful, fun personality. We both knew how to cook, no problem there. She also played a pretty good game of tennis and we used the college tennis courts a lot. It wasn't long until we had cadets lining up to challenge us to a game. We double dated a few of them. Neither of us knew that Jake had just met and started dating her younger sister Linda, whom he married years later.

WORLD WAR II

WE HAD BEEN AT WAR with Germany and Japan in World War II since December 8, 1941. I am ashamed to say now that many kids in rural areas were not aware of how bad things were then, and were not touched by having a close relative in the armed forces. No newspapers were delivered to us, there was no TV, and we did not listen to radio news very often. Movie news reels showed a few short items (if you happened to be in a theater); we heard very little discussion about it.

National "ration books, stamps and coupons" were distributed and monitored by the government during the war, in order that our armed forces could have the food, uniforms, boots, weapons, etc. they needed. Steel was scarce, gasoline, cigarettes, rubber tires (which were patched over and over again), soap, rayon stockings, and shoes with rubber soles were rationed, as were sugar, flour, coffee, meat, bread and many other staples and foodstuffs. Jake said that although farmers had their own food, they were monitored regularly, too. I was already gone from home when my family was concerned with this and was not as affected by it as others; I gave Mama most of my stamps.

I was in downtown Springfield with Mama and Dad one day during the summer of 1944. I had been attending Southwest Missouri State Teachers College as a freshman the year before, with the thought that I would continue my education and later go into teaching as so many girls did. I ran into one of the girls from my high school graduating class; her name was Gaileen. We visited for a while, catching up on our lives; I could see that she was very excited about something. She told me she had just signed up with a recruiter for a job at the Naval Ammunition Depot in Hastings, Nebraska, to start in a week or so.

We talked about it and she convinced me to ask my folks if I could go, too. The wages would be good and the work steady. We found Mama and Dad and after a short discussion, she took us all to see the recruiter where we learned more about it. I was so surprised and delighted that Dad and Mama agreed that it would be a good thing for me to do, although we didn't know how long it would be before I could come home.

Mama and I worked hard washing and ironing the clothes I would take, and we were busy buying sox and underwear and making new things such as pajamas, dresses, skirts, blouses, etc. Our uniforms would be furnished, so I didn't need work clothes.

At the appointed date and time, Gaileen and I boarded a U. S. Navy bus in town with our scarce belongings stuffed in pillow cases; we had never had a need for suitcases before. Our families hugged us and waved goodbye, and we started our trip to Hastings with the others who had been recruited, none of whom we knew. At our age, this was so different from what we had expected in our lives; we were so excited and a little apprehensive, looking forward to an adventure unlike any we had ever imagined.

I didn't know then that I would not see my Dad alive again.

It was a long, tiring ride with whatever sleep we could manage sitting up on the bus. We finally arrived in Hastings, tired and worn out from the rough bus ride, but anxious to see our final destination. We were taken directly to the base, and entered a room crowded with others in the same situation. Hastings was not a big town, even then, and it would be several hours before we would even see the city itself.

The Naval Ammunition Depot was some distance from the heart of that small town, set apart from everything else. It was surrounded by large earthen berms, which supported tall, sturdy, lighted, heavy wire fences atop concrete walls. Our bus entered through a guarded iron gate, manned with uniformed young men called Marines. There were many sailors moving about there, too. We were too young, inexperienced and "country" to have any idea about what we were getting into, but everyone on the bus was busy looking out the windows and buzzing about what we were seeing.

We were unloaded at a large gymnasium-type building with many American flags flying in the wind outside, mounted on tall sturdy poles. We entered in a single file and sat down in seats facing a wall fronted with an American flag, and covered by large maps of the world and a blackboard filled with information and instructions. After a somewhat lengthy interview where we filled out questionnaires, we were all finally assigned to certain ammunition lines.

Gaileen and I were assigned together, as had been promised by our recruiter; we would be working on the 40 MM shell line; for some reason they made me an inspector. They gave us maps and information about the town and surroundings. We were to start work the next week, a couple of days away.

Finally, we were taken downtown on our bus to a large three-story apartment building that was divided into very plain accommodations consisting of a room and an attached bathroom; there were two closets, two double bunk beds, two chests of drawers, and two fairly large desks with lamps. A "community" living room with couches, chairs, tables, lamps, a radio, and shelves with books and magazines was nearby down a hall, as was a laundry room.

Our roommates had beaten us to the lower bunks and were working at the plant; Gaileen and I climbed the ladders into the upper bunks, exhausted and ready for sleep. There was a cafeteria in our building and we would be having our breakfasts there.

Gaileen went to work on the assembly line, and I was taken to class for instructions on my job as an inspector. I had never even heard of a 40MM shell, had never seen a picture of one, had no idea of how it was used, and was glad that after some study, we would be accompanied by our instructors for a few days. The 40s were shipped to the Ammunition Depot almost completely assembled;

we finished them with their warheads, packaged them and shipped them out. I was so excited when I saw them later in a newsreel at a movie house, being used on a large ship, and I felt I had been of some use.

During our stay in the apartment, we found that our roommates had been wearing our clothes. The dead give-away was the orange color our clothes and shoes had picked up. The girls were assigned to the TNT line, and when we saw them, we were struck by the orange color of their hands, hairline at the temples, and their clothes. We found them to be very nice, fun people, except for their "borrowing" habit.

Gaileen and I were delighted when we were finally called in and told that we would be moving into an apartment in the basement of a home owned by an older couple in a nice neighborhood. The basement was furnished with a stove, a refrigerator, table and chairs and had a living room of sorts with a divan, chairs, tables and lamps. We had a small shower (heated water!) enclosed with a shower curtain. Our sleeping area was walled off from the living room with drapes all around and included a double bed, long dresser with mirror and a small nightstand with a lamp. We would have our own telephone. We were eager to move in. We met some people at work that lived nearby and managed to get a ride to and from work with them.

At work, we wore gray cotton coveralls--long sleeved, full length--and white sox with our heavy brown oxfords. We did not get to choose our uniforms for the day; they were handed out at random, no matter the size of the female or uniform--we took what we were given for the day. We could exchange the uniforms amongst ourselves if we wanted to do so. There were all ages and sizes of women working; there were all sizes of uniforms which buttoned up the front and had belts. We belted them in and thought we looked pretty good, until we completely covered our hair with the hair nets and white cotton bandanas that were also furnished. We were a pretty sight!!

The uniforms had to be dropped off the shoulders for bathroom visits, which was a little unhandy. Laundering of them was done on the base each day and clean uniforms were handed out the next day.

Sometimes on our breaks, one girl would get behind another in one large jumpsuit and try to walk or dance around. At other times, we would hang on one behind another in a long line and snake around the break room.

We showered after the day's work, all together in a big round shower in the center of one huge room. At first, I mostly faced the walls; I had never been exposed to seeing other girls and women naked and was embarrassed at first for the older, heavier women there. It was not too long, though, until we were all one big happy family and didn't pay any attention to each other in that regard. We sang together most of the time, and just generally got acquainted through talking.

We worked night shifts for a month, changed to day shifts for a month, etc. At first it was very confusing; it was hard to get used to the changes, but we were young so it didn't take long to adjust. There wasn't much to do except sleep after our night shifts, but we had lots of fun when we pulled day shifts. I sent a very modest amount of money home to Mama for her to use as needed. I do not remember filling out tax forms, or paying any income taxes.

Girls were still not wearing slacks, jeans, sweats or any type of long pants yet off the base. I spent some of my time and money buying material for a new dress now and again, and rented a used Singer sewing machine; these sewing machines were not electric, but still had the foot treadle like the one I had used at home. Many of our dresses had sweetheart necklines, were fitted around the waist, and had flared, gored skirts which came to the knees. We took liberties with the design of the sleeves, at least. Mama had taught me well how to adjust and mix patterns. I remember buying a lovely ready-made dressy black dress for special occasions.

As was the style then, we sometimes pinned onto the left shoulders of our dresses small artificial flowers that looked like corsages, worn not only at dances but also for dinner out, church or any dress-up occasion.

We wore very little make-up, mine was merely a fine face powder and a touch of rouge; mascara was not yet the "in" thing. We wore our hair long and mostly curly at the ends, never bleached then nor permed. We slept with 1" to 1-1/2" hair rollers in our hair. I did use Ponds or Lady Esther face cleanser at night. There weren't many choices for shampoos, deodorants, perfumes, etc., no hand lotions as now and no blow dryers. Today's young girls can't even imagine this, I'm sure.

Our dress shoes were very plain pumps, some had 2-inch heels which were almost as wide as high; some shoes were sling back. All were one of four colors--white, black, brown or navy; we could buy fancy little clip-on bows to dress them up. We were barelegged much of the time or used leg "paint", so that we didn't have to keep pulling up those saggy, heavy rayon hose when we danced!

I don't remember my heavy coat; I would have needed one for the frigid Nebraska winters. I do remember that we wore head scarves because of the wind--woolen in the wintertime. We had fancy knitted rayon or cotton scarves called snoods in beautiful colors that we wore on our heads for dress occasions.

There were USO dances several times a week, held in that big gymnasium. We danced to great live bands, sometimes servicemen, sometimes civilian bands hired to entertain us. We were encouraged and welcome to attend those and bring another girl. There weren't nearly enough girls there to go around for dancing partners for all the servicemen-- Navy, Marines, Coast Guard, and Air Corps.

It was more fun to go stag and dance with many guys than to go with a date. We many times each had our own long line of partners; we girls didn't stop dancing, just changed partners as they cut in on each other. Some from the same crew would surround a girl and take turns dancing with her. We met so many nice young men there, but really didn't date that much because of our working on the night shifts.

Gaileen met a nice Marine and not long after meeting, they became engaged. We double dated some. He was shipped elsewhere and she returned home to Rogersville. After they had been married for a while and living in Springfield, he was killed in a terrible accident while unloading large telephone poles from a flatbed railcar.

Shortly after she left, I was transferred to the depth charge line for a while--barrels filled with TNT that were rolled off the decks of ships into the ocean--then to a different shell line. When I left the 40s line, someone gave me an unloaded 40 MM shell for a souvenir, which I kept for many years after the war.

I worked for a while on the rocket line, which was manned with crazy fun-loving "Coasties", young men in the Coast Guard. That was a very different experience. They seemed to be totally unfazed by any impending danger. They laughed and played, sang and joked and tossed the rockets back and forth to each other; I think it was done partly to see how badly they could scare me. I tried to be nonchalant, but it did frighten me quite a bit.

At one time it became very quiet up and down the line and it was just a few minutes until I knew why. One of them had blown up a balloon (I hoped it was a balloon because I didn't know any better) and stuck it in a hole on the top of a rocket shell. I quietly removed it and shook my finger at them. I really didn't know what they expected from me, but they laughed and hooted for a bit.

Some shell assembly lines had below-grade tunnels to use for walking and for shipping the shells from one phase to the next; shells were loaded, upright, into metal containers and sent on conveyor tracks to the next phase of their assembly. The containers rumbled and squeaked as they moved along the tracks; many times I was alone with them for quite a spell as I walked from phase to phase of the inspection process.

I had heard shortly after my arrival there the rumor that one of the many tunnels had been badly damaged by an explosion inside it. No details were given, and we weren't sure it had really happened, but it was hard not to think about it as I walked quickly alongside them. I was always glad to reach my destination and get out of there safely!

Two of my new girlfriends moved into the apartment with me, two more moved into a bedroom upstairs, and our friendship continued. None of us wanted any part of "going steady" and we became very close friends.

We took turns visiting each other's churches on Sundays. We enjoyed learning about the differences in our religions, some were small differences. There was more confusion when we attended the Catholic Church, as much of the service was in Latin. I had never been to a Catholic Church before. There were Catholic Churches in Springfield itself, but none were located out in the small towns near us.

By now, we had met many young people, mostly servicemen. I often dated a really nice, gentle, thoughtful, dark-haired, brown-eyed sailor that was quite possibly the most handsome guy I had ever seen, especially when he was dressed in his perfect smile and his navy blue bell-bottom uniform, but he wanted to go steady and that was not my thing. He insisted on taking me to the dances but was content to sit on the sidelines and wait to take me home after. Was there something wrong with him, or with me for passing up a great guy like this? I just wasn't ready to be tied down.

One afternoon three of our Air Force friends came to our apartment, bringing with them three white Leghorn chickens, freshly beheaded (we didn't ask any questions). I seemed to be the only one who knew what to do with them--maybe the others were smarter than I about admitting it.

We boiled some water and I showed them how to scald the chickens and remove the feathers, how to singe off the fine hairs that were left, and how and where to cut for wings, legs, breasts and other parts; I'm not sure any of them absorbed these lessons or cared. It also fell to me to do the frying, but the others did whip up some mashed potatoes, etc. None of them admitted to knowing how to make gravy, either. Anyway, we had a lot of laughs and it was good eatin'. Mama would have been proud of me.

I had lived a protected life in warm secure neighborhoods all my life, with gentle, polite, respectful people, and was not afraid to be around strangers or nodding acquaintances. I was totally unprepared for the time that I had to ask for a ride home with some of the civilian men who carpooled to work on the line I was assigned to; they said they would be glad to take me home. I sat in the middle of the front seat between the driver and another man; three men sat in the back.

The man in the middle of the back seat leaned forward, put his hands down the back of my seat and managed to unhook my bra through my blouse. He went no further; he and the others laughed at my discomfort; I was livid! I gritted my teeth, I'm sure my face was red with anger, and I said nothing but sat as rigidly straight and stiff as I could with my arms crossed tightly over my chest until I was dropped off at home. Thankfully, he was only teasing me.

I never saw them again and was grateful for that. I never received any apologies from any of them and wouldn't know them now.

On the evening the war was declared ended, after atomic bombs Little Boy had been dropped on Hiroshima, Japan, on August 6, 1945, and Fat Man had been detonated over Nagasaki, Japan, on August 9, 1945, everyone in and around Hastings and the servicemen stationed there congregated downtown, screaming, yelling, laughing, and crying with joy and relief. No details had been given yet to the public there.

My girl friends and I were there in the middle of that mass of people. The few people who had cars drove slowly through the crowd. A convertible with the top down drove up next to us; two or three sets of strong hands reached out and grabbed me under the arms and lifted me into the car, screaming and kicking. It took only a minute to determine that they were Marines, happy Marines, celebrating! I don't know why I wasn't scared; I guess it was because I had met so many of them and had found them to be gentlemen and so much fun. They tried unsuccessfully to grab up another girl.

We slowly drove around for quite some time, joining the celebrators; after a while they took me to their mess hall and left me there with one of them, while the rest drove back out to the celebration. He was such a gentleman and I was not scared, although I learned later that my friends were quite frantic with worry. He cooked thick steaks and baked potatoes and made a salad and it turned out to be a very enjoyable evening getting acquainted with a nice, fun guy.

He took me home in a big flatbed truck where my friends met us with hugs and tears of relief.

We made a date, which included my friends, for the next weekend; we joined him and his baseball buddies on that big flatbed truck loaded with food and cokes. We spent many hours with them, cheering loudly, at their baseball games in the little towns around Hastings, where they played against local rag-tag teams. We met them at dances, etc., nothing serious, just good, clean fun. At other times, when they didn't have a scheduled game, we played baseball with them on a diamond in town.

Not long after the war was over, my friends and most of the workers were sent home. I stayed a while. I don't have a clue as to what was done with all the "left over" ammunition we had assembled in that once-busy place. Although I was extremely thankful, I felt completely lost. I had no idea about what I was going to do. Gradually, the men in the armed services were transferred to other places or received their discharges, and much of the life of the town of Hastings seemed to go with all of them.

When they let me go, I found a job at the Singer Sewing Machine Co. where I was well-known already after so often spending time and money there. I worked there for a few months before I finally packed up and took the train back home where again Orene picked me up. I dreaded seeing my home without my Dad. I had a sad reunion with all my family; we hugged, we laughed, and we cried as we reminisced about Dad. Somehow life went on. I didn't see my wartime friends again.

HEART-BREAKING LOSSES

It was bedtime. John was already in bed. We had been watching a sad drama on television and now I sat on the bathroom stool and suddenly began to cry. I put my elbows on my knees and held my face in my hands and I felt my hot tears run down my cheeks and over my fingers. Just all of a sudden, I thought of my parents, long, long gone now. Never a day goes by that I don't have tears in my eyes when I think of Mama and Dad and wish I could just hold them tightly and tell them how much I always loved them and "thanks" for such a good start to my life.

Dad died December 3, 1944, while I was in Hastings, Nebraska, working at the Naval Ammunition Depot. In addition to his farming, he had been a Road Superintendent for the Missouri Highway Department for a few years. He and Mama were in Springfield at the time.

I was at home in my apartment in Hastings when my cousin Orene Cowan called me from down home in late afternoon with the news. I hung up the phone and fell sprawled out on my stomach on the floor and cried my heart out. Nothing in my life up to then had ever hurt me so much nor prepared me for this kind of pain. I thought I was going to die, it hurt so much. I was only nineteen; I wasn't ready to lose my Dad! It was rumored that he died of food poisoning

from that day's lunch on the job, but I don't know for sure-
-none of his co-workers had trouble. Much later, someone
suggested it may have been diverticulitis, but that was never
confirmed to me.

When my boyfriend came that day, he found me still on
the floor and helped me make arrangements to go home to
Springfield on the train. It was filled with both servicemen
and civilians traveling for Christmas. I sat for hours on my
suitcase at the back of the crowded railroad passenger car,
stunned, tearful, and hurting. I don't remember how I got
through the long trip home, or if I even ate anything. Orene
picked me up at the train station and drove me home to the
farm. Many, many people were there--relatives, neighbors
and other friends, and several of his highway co-workers
came, filling the house and the yard. The temperature was
in the low eighties in early December.

Dad was laid out in his open coffin in the parlor; he had
been dressed in his one suit (black), a white shirt and a black
tie; he wore these things to funerals. I stood by his coffin,
my hands on his, and touched my lips to his cold cheek
as tears flooded my eyes and fell onto his face. Someone
came and gently guided me away. For a few minutes his
kids sat together in a tight circle in the side yard of the
house where we had had so much fun with him. We cried
quietly as we hugged each other. Mama was surrounded by
relatives, neighbors, friends; even so, I know she felt very
lost and alone.

His funeral was held in our yard, the yard where we had had
so much fun with him. I lived through those few sorrowful
days in a daze of my own, crying, hugging, acknowledging

sympathy from friends and relatives. I was devastated, inconsolable. I can't imagine that I was of any comfort to my mourning Mama or to my heartbroken brothers and sisters. The preacher lauded both Dad and Mama for our positive upbringing. We buried him in the Fulton Cemetery with his parents, brother, other relatives and friends where I can visit him and Mama when I'm down home.

There was food everywhere--fried chicken, ham, roasts, meatloaf, vegetables, salads, desserts of all kinds. Many people stayed at our home for several hours, trying to console us all. Impossible. We were so young; he was too young to go and had so much to live for. After a couple of weeks or so, I returned by train to Hastings to work. For days I was so angry with everyone there! How could they work, laugh, even talk? They knew my Dad had just died! It took me a long time to accept the facts and start to recover. Nothing and no one was any fun for a long, long while. The war ended not too long after that; he would have been so thankful.

I have wished many times that he could come back and spend time with his children now, together with our families, his grandchildren. He would be very pleased, but so sorry that his little red-headed Russ is gone. I wish he had lived to enjoy the changes that have been made in airplanes, in cars, trucks, and farm machinery such as huge air-conditioned combines, threshing machines and tractors that make his small Farmall seem like a toy. He would enjoy so much watching with us the baseball and basketball games and the news on television. Many people believe he can see these things.

Mama survived.   She must have missed Dad so very, very desperately after he died so young.   She took on the responsibility of raising their kids alone and did a truly wonderful job of it. Neighbors and kinfolks were always there for her.

Jake and Wade were old enough and were well-trained by Dad to handle the necessary chores, although the long trips for buying livestock to be fattened up for sale were now over. Jake and Wade and the other kids all pitched in to do what they could in the summertime. When the others were in school and were gone almost all day, it was up to Jake to be the man of the family during those times. He took over many of the chores, planting and harvesting what he could by himself until Wade, Weldon and the other kids came home from school to help.

They grew to be "men" before their time and Dad would have been so very proud of them.

Mama put her land in a government program (AAA - Agricultural Adjustment Administration) for farmers that allowed them not to plant, and draw a small stipend for not doing so. This program was one of the New Deal agencies set up by President Franklin D. Roosevelt and was a lifesaver for her and her family. She also sold a few acres of her land. Presently, the price of land around that part of the state has sky-rocketed and if Dad and Mama had lived a little longer, they would be well-off enough to sit back and enjoy the fruits of their labors.

Since I was in Nebraska, it was up to Barb, at thirteen, and Fran, at nine, to be Mama's little helpers in the home. Mama saw that everyone carried out their duties and she raised them to be responsible adults. I still mourn for my funny, funny dad, and for my brave, loving mother, who did such a wonderful job of raising her children under such stressful circumstances. Their faces dance before my closed, teary eyes many times before I fall asleep at night.

Several years after Dad's death, when most of us kids were gone and involved in our own adult lives, she reluctantly decided she didn't need the problems of a big house any more. She sold the old home place to a man, Clarence Lackey, and his wife and children. This family tore down the old house shortly thereafter, built a fine new home on the grounds and lived there for a short time. They left the barn, silos and other buildings standing. At first, it was a sad feeling to go down there after she moved from our old home place, strange to see another family living in the home we had lived in for so long. Grandpa must have looked down and cried.

They sold it then to a man named John Dominy and his wife and kids. Mama enjoyed this lovely family for many years, watching the children grow up. He recently died but his wife is still there, although she is in ill health. One of their girls built a nice home on the front forty acres across the road from Wade.

Mama remodeled and built onto the little house across and down the road on the Christian County side that had been so many things to us. It was a different feeling to be visiting her on the old grain house property. She put in a bathroom, and refinished everything, painting, wall-papering, etc. She did a great job of making it a lovely, comfortable three-bedroom home in a beautiful setting for her to live in for lots of years. She planted flowers and flowering bushes around the home, put in a strawberry patch at the southeast corner and, with help from her kids, started a new garden plot, 'tho not nearly as large as her old one.

Teenagers Fran and Russell were there with her for a little while. Wade and his family had built a home just east of her, close by when she needed something. An old nearby storage building was made into a garage for her. She joined the Wolf Women's Club where she had and was a secret pal for a year at a time; they gossiped a little and discussed kids, grandkids, recipes, sewing, gardening, etc. She learned to drive and had one small wreck that bruised her up a bit.

Something bit her on the leg one day when she was working in the fencerow picking blackberries; it was something poisonous and her lower leg swelled to double size, was bruised and very painful. She had to have tetanus shots and took sulfa drugs; it was a long time healing. In spite of it, she was heard singing her songs.

Mama wasn't as busy now and gradually gained weight over the years, and it became more and more difficult for her to get around and "work", but we all were glad to see her slowing down some. She could still put together a quick complete meal for anyone that might drop in on her and she enjoyed doing it.

One week when I visited her, I drove into town and bought some concrete patio blocks, several bags of sand and a big bag of coarse gravel. (Rocks! I bought rocks! The millions of rocks we had on the farm were too big, so I bought rocks!) All by myself, in spite of her objections that it was too much for me to do, I put in a 12'x12' patio for her in the level part of her lawn in the shade of a tree just outside her kitchen door. It was a place where she could sit, many times peeling fruit, shelling peas or snapping green beans, or just enjoying nice weather, resting. She enjoyed it for many years and it made me so, so happy to have done it for her.

We had several of our family 4ths and Christmas celebrations in that house with her, crowded every year with more and more family additions--family Dad would have loved very much. She was a loving babysitter for her grandkids, although we found out later that they took advantage of her inability to get around as quickly as they, and their yelling was louder than her yelling, yet she never complained to us. Debbie said that to calm them down, she sometimes pretended to cry.

Now, many years later, I imagine her smiling face in front of me, both at "27"and in her later years, and I can imagine I hear her singing.

She had been our babysitter for a few days when Debbie was born. She visited us many times in Kansas City, and we took her and John's mother, Evelyn ("Sikes"), with us on many vacation trips, with a sleeping, small young Debbie spread across their laps in the back seat. We took them to Colorado, Arizona, California, Florida, etc. They bought large sacks of oranges and some souvenirs that we had to pack in the trunk with our baggage.

She enjoyed the bright lights and the commotion in Las Vegas; she watched the action as she leaned on the rail of the craps table with her large crossed arms covering too much of it until she was gently asked by the croupier to back off. She and Sikes sat on tall stools at a bar and had beers.

She was amazed at the fascinating colors and bubbling surfaces of Yellowstone National Park. She whooped with joy as she waded barefoot out into knee-high waves of the Pacific Ocean in California, lifting her skirt a little and feeling the sand shifting beneath her feet. John's mother kept her face turned toward the wall of the mountains we climbed and descended on narrow roads and, because she had been there before, told Mama not to be afraid, that everything would be okay, but Mama didn't want to miss any of the beautiful scenery she had never even had a reason to imagine.

John and I had driven down from Kansas City several times to visit Mama in St. John's Hospital in Springfield earlier when she was so sick, and went later when she was sent home at her request. She was in her mid 70's when she died. I miss her so very much and I wish I would have done more for her as did my brothers and sisters and their families who lived nearby.

After all these years I remember how much she loved us all and how much she sacrificed, although she didn't consider any of it to be a sacrifice. She was happy to be our Mama. She worked almost constantly for her family and set an excellent example of being a good mother, loving and understanding, reprimanding as necessary.

She was dressed in her Sunday best and was wearing the beautiful starburst "rhinestone" brooch that I had given her many years before for Christmas. I just felt I had to leave it with her and remember her that way. Her funeral was held on a day after several days when it had rained and rained and rained; her grave filled with water and burial was delayed for almost an hour while some neighbors pumped out the water. People stayed inside the church after the service, waiting to go to the burial; there were flowers everywhere; there were so many people there and at her home later where family and friends served food and told stories about her. I didn't feel like eating anything.

She had put away some money to pay for her funeral. We "kids" sat in her living room the next day, crying and laughing while remembering events of past years, and asked everybody what they might want as a remembrance, maybe something they had given her as a gift, etc. She had very little, nothing certainly to fight over. She had no attic full of antiques, there was no jewelry made with exotic or precious jewels or gold.

She had an aqua green four-door sedan that she had bought from Jerry's wife sometime earlier, and we all decided that Russ's wife, Mary, should have it and learn to drive. I still have a few of the little gifts she gave me through the years, many of which she made herself, and I won't part with them yet; they remind me every day of the love we had for each other. Debbie was fascinated by the quilts Mama had made and Mama had given her one as a remembrance.

My brothers and sisters have remained very close through the years. Weldon and Jeanne live farthest away in Georgia,

John and I live in Overland Park, Ks., but the others have settled in not too many miles from home; Jake and Linda lived in Ozark for many, many years before they died, as have Fran and Joe. Wade (Shirley, his wife of so many years just recently died) is still in the house close to where Mama lived, and Barb and Davy are but a mile away, across from the old Wolf School location. Mary is still in Springfield.

Some of our kids are near there and some scattered into other places. We all try to celebrate Christmas together in one home or another on a date as close to Christmas as we can get, and we try to get as many of us together as we can around July 4, including our children and their several new babies.

Annabelle still lives nearby as do Bonabeth and Kathryn, Hazel lives near Mama's old home place, Aunt Pad's Anita is in Florida and Kiddo's Anita is still in Arizona. Kathleen is in a rest home in Ozark. Hooge and Jerry's kids and grandkids are in and around Springfield, I've heard.

I think I'll go back down there soon and give Wade a spanking for old time's sake, tote Barb on a bike ride, go with Weldon to some barn to see how many times he can fall over something, have Fran bake me a deeeelicious gooseberry pie and tell Mary a cute joke just to see her laugh. Then a trip to the old Fulton cemetery would be in order, to visit silently and lovingly with Dad & Mama, Russ, Shirley, Jake and Linda and their baby girl, as well as others who are long gone now.

LIFE GOES ON AND ON AND ON, THEN....

At first I loved the Microwave oven; it was so convenient for a working mom; it took so little time to accomplish a task and it was an easy cleanup--very handy. Now, I'm not so sure I like it. I only have to punch a button or two for the time it will take to defrost, warm or cook something, but it's the "time" that bothers me. Those seconds and minutes go by so fast and show me that some of the precious minutes I have left in my life are counting down.

"Time" for a baby is measured first in womb months, then in days, weeks, then months and on into toddler years. At 5 or 6, their ages are measured in school years and so on into high school where they are called "teeners". Time passes quickly with all the things they want or have to do, all the things they have to get in on--so much to learn, so many people to meet, so many places to go and new things to try, but it concerns them only when there is not enough of it to do all the fun things they plan. Then come the working years and on into their own family "together" time.

Not until I turned 79 then 80 did it dawn on me that I have so little precious time left with all the people I love.

I plan to make the most of it, enjoying family and friends, wonderful caring neighbors, trips to new and old places, sunrises and sunsets, blue skies with white clouds, gentle rains, beautiful flowers and the relaxing it takes to be able to enjoy all of these things. I feel so very lucky to have had this life with these people for so long a time!

I find now that I was unwittingly storing all kinds of things in a young memory box deep inside my brain: The feel of satiny fine dust underneath my bare feet and rising between my toes, smells of new hay in the barn loft, different smells in different parts of the barnyard, the silky feel of new chicks, meals being prepared in a country kitchen by a mother singing Dutch songs in words unfamiliar to me, a refreshing quiet rain hitting dusty paths and perking up colors of nature's beautiful flowers and plants, the same rain cooling too-hot bodies on a summer day--so many things I took for granted.

These memories are being brought to life now as I put words on paper, one memory leading to another--love we took for granted, fun in green grass or deep snow or maybe lying peacefully under a tree looking up into clear blue skies with white clouds, feeling the warmth of Spring after a cold long wintertime.

I recall the feel of Mama's warm arms around me as I sat on her ample lap, yielded later to younger siblings, their yielding to the next family addition and joining me at the foot of her rocking chair--these feelings not really forgotten, just stored away in a grateful heart.

Putting these memories down on paper has been such a rewarding experience for me, flooding my brain and heart with pictures and feelings of love and thankfulness for having been born into this particular loving family, in this uncomplicated place and time, in this country I love so much. I can't even imagine any other life and am grateful to God for all he has given me in my so-far 80-plus years.

This is not our story alone; it is the story of families like ours, living out their day-to-day lives simply, sometimes harshly, sometimes filled with giddy happiness and sometimes with deep, deep sorrow and great losses. Different things will be remembered by city, small-town folk and farmers, rich or poor or in between, along with their individual joys and downtimes. Many of my friends relate in some way to this story, and my family is appreciative of my writing it down for them and theirs.

While we were at our winter home in a trailer park in Mesa, Arizona, I mentioned to a new friend from Canada my writing my life story and she asked to read it. She and I were amazed at the similarities of our early lives, growing up so far apart--same values, even some of the same recipes. She marked off a narrow column on the right side of each page and made comments about like things and question marks about unlike things. Of course, there were some differences which we discussed and we had a good laugh at them. We laughed, too, at the differences in the way we expressed ourselves in a conversation.

Some time has passed since I started our story, with much help from family members. We are more and more thankful that so much of our special family group is still intact.

In addition to losing Red Russell at such an early age, we have recently lost three more precious members. We lost our oldest brother, Jake, in late August, 2009, and his wife, Linda, died November 29, 2009. Wade's wife, Shirley, died in February, 2009. We will miss them terribly.

Yes, some of us are lacking most of the energy and skills of our former years; nonetheless, we are glad to have each other still around in any shape or form, and thoroughly and lovingly enjoy all the additions. We do miss the July 4 ball games at Barb and Davy's, but enjoy the swimming pool and fun at Chris and Vicki's instead.

Yes, too, the old home place is long gone now except in the thoughts and hearts of those of us who still are alive and have such fond deep memories of our young lives spent there among all of these people who were so very dear to us at a time when morals and loyalties were important for building decent, loving futures. I wouldn't change any of it, certainly none of my beloved family.

The family tree thing didn't work for us; after all the time spent getting it together, most copies were stuck away in a drawer somewhere. I encourage someone in all families to start a family history story; they will be amazed at all the help they will get from others ....until the "others" are gone and no longer have input!!!!!! It is a "do it now!" thing.

THE FAMILY GROWS
AND GROWS UP

Mama was the shortest of our immediate family at 5' 3" tall; Dad was 6'2 or 3", probably taller when he was younger. Barb ended up being the shortest of us kids, about 5'5"; I was 5'8" tall as a young woman and Fran was just a little taller. Almost every Christmas or Fourth we take a picture of us by age and then by height.

Russ was the shortest brother at about 5'10", Weldon is a few inches taller, and Jake and Wade are several inches over 6'. Fran's husband Joe and kids are all tall – Lance is way up there at 6"5" and Jack towers over him a little bit; Diana is 5'9". She's the youngest grandchild and Debbie is the oldest.

June met John Ketterer Ellis when she attended Chillicothe Business College after the war was over. He had been in the Army Air Corps during World War II. He was one of five young men who came to Chillicothe from Odebolt, Iowa. They were married on October 19, 1947, in Kansas City, Mo., and stayed in the Kansas City area except for about five years living at the Lake of the Ozarks.

They both worked for Shefrin Sales Company for several years. John worked for several additional firms, mostly in sales, including thirty years with Aylward Products Co. John and Weldon spent some time in Attica, N.Y. gunniting, inside and outside, the 31' tall prison walls there. June later worked in K.C. for the government on the F-101 Jet project, and later at Bendix on a project for the Navy.

They moved to Johnson County, Kansas, where their daughter, Debra, was born June 29, 1954. Debbie graduated from Emporia State College in Emporia, Kansas, and is very bright, very, very funny. She worked for 18-plus years for the Sprint Corporation in the human resources department, and works now for the Better Business Bureau. Both June and John are retired, although John still sells a blade or two.

Jake resembled Dad a lot in his own way, tall with dark hair. On January 1, 1948, he married Linda McNeil, a dark, pretty girl from Walnut Grove, Mo. I roomed with her sister, Freda, when I attended SMS and we didn't know Jake and Linda had even met. Linda is from a family even larger than ours and I have met many of them.

Jake and Linda lived in Ozark, Mo. where Jake managed the Oldsmobile-Chevrolet dealership for many years until his retirement. Jake was in the U.S. Air Force for four years, stationed at Whiteman Air Base, Knobnoster, Mo., during the Korean Conflict and spent some time in England. Jake died in late August, 2009, in a rest home in Ozark where he lived with Linda for a few months and their home and furnishings have been sold at auction.

Their first daughter, Janice Lynne, was stillborn and is greatly mourned even now. Their daughter Tracy met Gary Davis and they were married in Hawaii. They live near Jake and Linda; Tracy is a horse lover and they own many beautiful Arabians of different ages. She has had a few accidents with them, but has never lost her love of horses. They have two teensy little dogs they enjoy showing off. She and Gary have a business selling lemonade refreshments at Branson, Missouri, and keep very busy in the summertime. She also works full time for United Parcel.

Wade met and married Shirley Jean Sheppard of Springfield. Wade worked many years for Harding Glass Co. in Springfield, and recently retired from there. Shirley worked for several doctors in Springfield. They built a home just down the road from the old farm place, yes, just past the hollow on the way to the mailbox and over the underground river that manufactures sinkholes. He looks a lot like Dad, but in a different way, and is gentle and laid-back in attitude; no wonder Shirley was always smiling. She just recently died in February, 2009, and we miss her terribly.

Wade raises hunting dogs and is a crack shot--the birds don't have a chance. He can brag about a beautiful garden every year. He is handy at fixing anything and is called back to work to cut and install mirrors and glass in windows for neighbors and former customers, and in the aftermath of tornadoes and other storms or fires in nearby communities. As far as I know, he no longer gets so many spankings, and the record he set may still be intact.

Their daughter, Vicki, and her husband, Chris Chastain, live very nearby on the road south towards the old "lower place"; they have two children: Amanda, a lovely young lady with a ready smile who is very good with the younger kids in the family, and Tyler Wade who has eyes that shine with fun when he smiles at you and is a very bright young man – bright as he is handsome!

Barb married her childhood sweetheart, Davy Lee Hale, in 1950. They live across the road from where the old Wolf grade school house was. He has been a Shriner for many years. They had the service station/deli on Highway 60 toward Springfield, the most popular place to stop for gas, eats and visiting. They have many tales to tell of their experiences there, such as the day the hippies cleaned out their van in the station drive right in the front door! Davy made them clean it up and put it back in the van and told them to leave – now! They both work part time now in Cody, another station down the road – forget the ownership problems! Davy and his brother, Ray, were stationed in Germany in 1951-53 during the Korean Conflict.

Barb and Davy have two sons, Greg and Johnny, both musically inclined. Greg married Lori Samuels, a former childhood neighbor, in 1999, and they have one little boy, Mason Dean, cute, cute, cute, one of the youngest of our family, born in August, 2000. He's a very smart little boy and is in grade school now; he has always been the spittin' image of Greg when he was little. He has quite a collection of dinosaurs and many, many little cars. He is a natural on the computer.

They lived in Overland Park, Ks. for a few years when Greg worked at the Olathe Air Control Center where he told pilots when and where or where not to go; of course, it was more serious than that, being an air controller. They moved recently to a beautiful new home they built on a farm near their folks in Rogersville. He had a lot of help from his brother Johnny, and Lori has done a lovely job decorating it

Greg plays piano in a band for fun, and keeps busy doing it for parties and in nightclubs. He is a computer whiz and graciously helps out us old folks with ours. He works occasionally at his old job as an air controller. Lori sells all kinds of beautiful wrought iron pieces, handbags and jewelry.

Johnny works at the Federal Penitentiary Hospital in Springfield and has many tales to tell about the famous tough prisoner-patients there. He married Lisa McKenzie in 1988 and they have three children: Brandon, a handsome but shy, smart boy with beautiful eyes, Whitney, a little girl full of fire, vim and vigor getting prettier every day, and Logan, a darling little boy who loves to entertain us with his singing--and you'd better pay attention!! Lisa is a grade school teacher and their kids know lots of things already. They live in a beautiful new home near her folks and near Barb and Davy. Johnny, Davy, Greg, and friends helped with many parts of the building of it.

Weldon was in the Coast Guard in 1952-55, traveled to many, many places, and has interesting stories to tell about that part of his life. He graduated as an engineer from Rolla School of Mines in Rolla, Mo. He was working for Western Waterproofing Co. in Kansas City, Mo., with my husband John when they were sent on a job to Attica, N.Y., to gunnite the prison walls inside and out, about 31' tall.

While there, in 1955, he met Jeanne Emily Austin and they were married in 1956. They now live in a lovely home in Quitman, Ga. where he can raise his beautiful flowers to his heart's content, when he isn't doing part-time consulting and traveling.

He and Jeanne have moved around the eastern part of our country a lot because of his work--many cities, many states--and he has traveled to consult with companies in China, Japan, India, and many other places overseas. He relates to us very interesting stories about experiences in those countries. When John and I went with the Chargers to Tokyo, we stayed in the same hotel Weldon had stayed in on his trips there; we didn't know it until we got back home.

Mama said that he resembled her handsome father, but we have no pictures to prove it. He wouldn't talk much until he was three or four years old--he did talk a lot to the chickens, though. When he was five or six he wouldn't shut up. Dad's patience was astounding when Weldon followed his every step asking "why?", "why?", "why?" As he was growing up, he was inquisitive enough that he took apart radios and anything else that would come apart to see what made them tic. He is still a man of many questions with his inquisitive mind, and to this day he is still asking "why?", "why?", "why?" and can give you many answers if you ask "why?"

Weldon and Jeanne have four children. Desiree Jean is married to Mark Taylor and they lived in Omaha, Nebraska, in a beautifully restored old home, with their two daughters, dark, pretty girls, Fiamma Jean and Isabella for many years.

They recently moved to Council Bluffs, Iowa. Our local families feel we do not see them often enough but enjoy receiving their pictures. Mark manufactures and erects garages. Frankie Weldon is a computer whiz living near Weldon and Jeanne, he was married, then divorced and has no children. Victor Austin lives nearby, too, having moved from Ridgewood, N.J., and Darcy has an interior decorating shop in Quitman, Ga., full of beautiful items of all kinds.

Frannie is married to Joe Brazeale; Debbie was a flower girl at their wedding in 1960. They were each stag when they met at a little beer garden and dance hall, Tony's, in Springfield. When they finally got together, after he called her for a date and she was on vacation, they dated for almost two years. They live on a farm near Ozark, Missouri, and have several stock animals. Fran was a seamstress for many years altering men's clothing in a store in Springfield after retiring from another job. Joe is retired from his job as a supervisor at Harding Glass Company. They have done extensive traveling overseas since his retirement-- Russia, Germany and other countries.

Their older son, Lance, married Lesa Marshall on June 21, 1995, in Grand Cayman Island, and they live in a lovely home in Shawnee, Kansas, overlooking the Kaw River. Both are air controllers in Olathe where Greg worked-- the three of them kept the planes in line, in the air, and almost on time! They both attended the University of Missouri, but did not meet until they were working at the traffic center. They have a handsome son, Little Joe, who is in grade school.

Jack, their next son, recently married a fun girl, Jennifer, who is in sales. They have a farm home near Fran and Joe, and across the fields from that of Tracy and Gary down south of Ozark. Jack also works for Harding Glass. Jack has always enjoyed sitting, listening and laughing as others joke around; Jennifer has a wonderful sense of humor and is very loving and is a good cook; she is a wonderful influence for Jack.

Diana, tall and pretty, is a lawyer living in Ozark, Missouri, is fun to be around and is as smart as a whip, although she and I drive Debbie crazy playing scrabble--she and I are never ready ahead of time. She worked in a law firm in the K.C. area for a spell and lived in Overland Park, Kansas, for a time.

Russell married Mary Mareno in 1959 and they lived in Springfield for a while where their four kids were born. Russ had his own floral shop there, where he also sold many different styles of lovely accessory pieces, both for the home and the yard. Over the years, he ventured into silk flowers and was very successful with his beautiful arrangements. He loved to cook and always brought an interesting new dish to family gatherings. Mary was a nurse at St. Johns' Hospital until her retirement.

They moved to a farm just outside Halfway, Missouri, where they had a large yard with a pond; the kids went through high school there. We lost him to cancer in 1990, which just broke our hearts and we miss him dearly. After a year or so, Mary moved back to Springfield where she continued her nursing career and later remarried.

He and Mary have Monte, redheaded as was Russ, who married Anne Kolb in October, 2004, and they recently moved to Olive Branch, Mississippi. He works in Memphis for the U.S Customs Department. They are the parents of a handsome little boy, named Matthew Kent, born in June, 2006.

Carla lives in Richardson, Texas, near Dallas, and works in sales for Payment Tech., in credit card processing. She is a sweetheart and fun to be around, very loving.

April married David Nanos in 1995 and they live in Olathe, Kansas, not far from us. April worked as a physical therapist at North Kansas City Hospital and David works in advertising. She just recently went to work for Olathe Hospital to be nearer to her beautiful home. "Beautiful ready smile" describes her.

The third daughter, Amber, married Joey Hocut in 2003, who works in construction and siding, and she works for a food manufacturer. On July 19, 2005, they welcomed into their home their brand new baby boy; they named him Jett Russell. They live in Carl's Junction, Mo., near Joplin, in a nice home where Joey did a lot of renovating and Amber did a great job of decorating. In June, 2008, they lovingly welcomed a little girl, Jaisie. Absolutely DARLING children!

A BOY NAMED JOHN

I DIDN'T KNOW IT THEN, OF course, but as I was being born on November 27, 1925, a little boy in the small town of Odebolt, Iowa, was celebrating his first birthday on that same day. Who could have guessed that that little boy would grow up to be the man I would marry?

They named him John Ketterer (his mother's maiden name) Ellis (I call him now "Kettererer"); his nickname there was "Bush". His mother's name was Evelyn Nanice, nicknamed "Sikes" for some reason; his father's name was Earl Arthur, called "Bugs", and he was very active in the Masonic Lodge until his death. John had a sister, Kathleen, the first-born, who died of diphtheria at the age of one-year-plus. His sister, Gwynn, was six years older than he. There were many aunts, uncles and cousins.

John's grandmother Ellis visited them regularly every year. She was a wiry little woman who loved to chew tobacco. If she didn't have a fresh chaw handy, she broke open any cigarette butts that might be lying around that had been smoked down as far as possible without burning the fingers that held them. She unwrapped them and used the leftover tobacco for chewing. Sometimes John's mother left "lost" tobacco lying around for her to find, which made her day. Didn't matter; she lived into her mid-nineties.

Their home was a white two-story building on two lots near the downtown area; it had a fairly large yard. They had electricity and phone service. They had cold running water, and had oil-fired stoves for heat. There was one corner of the living room designated and furnished as the "parlor" and it was pretty much off-limits to John and his rowdy friends.

He always had a dog or two, and they slept with him under the covers in his upstairs bedroom and when he slept on the pull-down bed in the living room in the wintertime. They were mostly toy Manchesters and various mutts of mixed breeds at different times. One of his favorites was named "Boy"; one was "Wimpie", one was "Sport", one was "Pepper".

John was full of the joy of life from the beginning, always busy, jumping and running. He made the rounds of his neighbors, who gave him homemade cookies or Swedish bread with butter, and many times they invited him to sit down at their table to eat with them. At an early age, he and the other kids knew personally most of the people in town (and where to go for cookie handouts).

He also regularly visited the downtown stores, especially Charley Nelson's Variety Store where penny candy was kept in open containers on the countertop. One day when John had no pennies, he sneaked a couple of pieces into his pocket and walked out. Sylvester Lunkenhiemer, one of his good buddies, saw him take it and told Sikes about it. Sikes took John by the ear, marched him down to the store and made him pay for the candy, a lesson he has not forgotten to this day.

In the wintertime, baled hay was piled around the bases of the farm homes and up their outside walls for some protection. Eisenglas was tacked to the outside of the windows to keep out the cold wind. Many, many big trees, including evergreens for winter foliage, were planted around the northwest and north sides of the homes there. Snowfalls in Iowa were frequent, deep and long-lasting. The kids built forts and had snowball fights; they enjoyed their sleds in the park and on the slopes of the streets. They came in from play cold and wet; there were no nylon or down-filled outdoor clothes then....kids didn't know or care.

Many summers were extremely dry and hot. John remembers one 100-degree night during a drought year when he was a kid and had made his pallet inside the front screen door in the living room as he did so often then. He was sleeping and was awakened by a tire that rolled in through the screen door, but he was not hurt.

Across the street from his home was a park where he and his friends spent many, many hours. This land sloped slightly from the east to the west, which was great for sledding. The boys, with a little advice from dads or big brothers, constructed their own "racing cars" for home-made soap box derbies to be run on the street by that hill. One year the adults about fainted when the kids built a bonfire in the middle of the street and started driving the little "cars" through it--luckily, no one was hurt, but there was no more of that! Kids spent many, many hours together in the park in all of the months.

There were other things to do, such as biking and roller skating in the streets (skates clamped onto your shoes' soles then, no separate boots). There were neither skateboards nor inline skates.

John's folks, as far back as he can remember, took into their home, fed and cared for at different times young boys and girls who worked around town or went to school there during the Depression. John especially liked Ted Crum, who was several years older and was like an older brother to John. He stayed and worked there for several years and they kept in touch after he left.

His Mom always had a big garden; she canned foods and they were kept in the cellar. She had one fruit tree--a plum. She had to call one of the two town doctors one day because John swallowed several plums, seed and all, when he was a very young boy. He also put a handful of lye in his mouth one day when he was a toddler. They were lucky to have medical help nearby to make house calls on the elderly and ill, as there were many other close calls. The cellar was where Bugs made his homebrew; he had many bottles of it blow up.

His dad was the town barber, and John spent a lot of time in the barber shop and in the adjoining pool hall, where no woman was allowed to set foot, just as was true in many small towns. He wore white shirts with ties every day there. The parlor on the first floor was made into a bedroom for his Mom and Dad, but had no closets. There was a chest and a tall closet chest; his dad spread his dress pants out on the floor each night. Gwynn had a closet in her bedroom upstairs. There was no running water in the kitchen, but the toilet sink did have running water. John took his baths in a galvanized tub in the kitchen.

John had one suit (with knickers) ordered from Sears when he was very young, and had a suit for graduation.

One day when a young John had finished doing his regular cleanup work (such as it was) in the saloon, sweeping and cleaning the spittoons (he usually got paid with a candy bar), Bugs gave him a haircut. John still remembers that his dad began at the nape of his neck by making a big sweep with the clippers up over the top of his head. He sat very still throughout the cutting, then tore out running from the laughter, and didn't cry until he got home, then let out a loud howl! Things didn't get any better when his mom laughed.

In the mid 30's when John was a young, small boy, his dad sponsored--as a merchant in Odebolt--a "kittenball" team; this was another word for a softball team that traveled from town to town in Iowa. John was allowed to go to the games as a bat boy for the older players.

From the time they were born, one of John's best friends was Kelly "Beano" Smith, whose mom Clarissa was one of Sike's best friends; she ran a restaurant downtown. His Dad made a square hole in the ceiling and nailed boards to the wall for a ladder to go upstairs to the living area through a trap door. They later bought the hotel and opened a restaurant in addition to renting rooms. A few years later, she opened her own restaurant on the downtown main street.

These boys spent most of their time together through the years, even staying with each other during various childhood diseases and illnesses, and playing every day with other boys. One of these boys was Leo "Pee Wee" Simon, who was one of the funniest men I have ever met. Almost everyone in town had a nickname and everybody could mimic everyone else, and they did, with no hard feelings! Leo was the very best at it; he had their speech and their actions down pat.

John said he spent most of his time in grade school looking out the window. He did better on the playground and in the park across the street from his home than he did in the classroom.

When they were kids, John and Leo were asked to play a duet for the patients at a mental hospital in a neighboring town. Leo was to play the harmonica and John had the sweet potato. The stage curtain rose slowly; in front of them in the large room were many people lined up in chairs and beds staring at them and expressing in different ways their handicaps. Leo played his harmonica so well that they cheered and clapped them back for a repeat performance; John had frozen at the first sight of these unfortunate people, not one note came out. Same thing-- Leo played another solo--no backup sweet potato!

John's Uncle John Ketterer, Sike's brother, came through Odebolt almost every summer in the 30's from Flint, Michigan, on his way back to California with his latest new Buick, usually staying with them for a week or ten days. He had two daughters, Jackie and Nita, both gone now, and John enjoyed their visits very much and we saw them occasionally in later years.

When he was in high school and on the basketball team, John and two other players were asked to submit a nickname for the athletic teams. Because John's Uncle John was a rabid fan and sent him the Southern California football and other athletic teams' programs, John nominated the name "Trojans" and that name was picked--The Odebolt Trojans.

John's Uncle Joe Ketterer was a railroad depot agent; he was a master showman with a huge (6 inch) yo-yo and taught John many tricks, most of which he has since completely forgotten. His uncle had many other little tricks and gadgets and loved to entertain, many times standing on top of the railroad boxcar and throwing the yo-yo out as far as he could.

His Uncle Ray Ellis had two daughters, Jane (no longer with us) and June; June was always a favorite cousin to John. At one time they lived in Sioux City and John visited them there many times during his young years; they swam every day. John and June are still the best of friends and we visit her and her family yearly in their condo at a lake in Minnesota.

The first few times I visited Odebolt, I had a hard time understanding much of what some of them were saying, with their deep Swedish accents. I, of course, had the beautiful twangy Ozarkian slow talk; they called me a hillbilly and tried to talk the same as I. They couldn't get it quite right; you have to be raised around it, I guess--

the two syllables for one-syllable words, the youalls, etc. I took a lot of ribbing for it, but I couldn't talk to sound like them either.

One thing amazed me; many of their dishes had an entirely different taste and many of them were much like the ones at home in southern Missouri. With communications as they were, or were not, and very little interstate travel, how were the recipes the same?

Odebolt for a long time was known as the popcorn center of the world! That was one of many staples grown there, and there were several cribs owned by the Crackerjack Company used for storage of the popcorn ears before they were sent out to their processing plants in Chicago.

The Boyer River ran alongside the highway just east of town. River! Unlike those in the southern Missouri Ozarks, there were no trees and brush along its banks; one could have unknowingly walked right into it in the dark of night. It was shallow--field level, it had no gravel bottom, there were no big rocks or boulders in or alongside the stream, which should have been making several turns and meandering downhill through the fields. The people there called it a "river"! No boating, no fishing.

There was a large gravel pit nearby where the boys went swimming and diving. All were good swimmers except Leo; they kinda took turns throwing him in then "saving" him.

Five miles east of Odebolt was the town of Wall Lake (home of famous singer Andy Williams) one of Odebolt's athletic rivals; five miles east of that was another, Lake

View. Both lakes were kept very busy. Lake View had a large lake, with campgrounds available to the public.

John's family had a one-bedroom cottage named "Linger Longer" on the lake in Lake View where they spent a lot of time in the summer. The cottages were of various ages and sizes and were built next to one another a foot or two apart. There was a public beach and pier which was part of Lakewood Park. That area has changed considerably, with old, small, unheated, uninsulated cottages torn down and big modern homes and docks built recently. It is truly a beautiful area.

John and several of his friends called themselves the "Polecats" and they had a clubhouse in the garage of one of the Polecat member's parents a half block from downtown. It had one window and wooden floors; it also had a trapdoor into the wall of the attached cob house next door. They "borrowed" (with permission) the cobs for fuel for the small stove they had, which was vented to the outside. They had a small table and chairs, and a double bed they made for themselves to nap on or use to stay overnight. They learned to smoke there, some roll-your-owns and some real cigarettes, filched wherever they could be found.

One day John and Charley Craig painted Joey Craig's face with red enamel--very painful and hard to remove. Nothing they tried or did was a surprise to their folks. Leo's younger brother, Pauly, "Mooch", was put close to the end of a catch basin adjoining a manhole by the creek. The boys poured gasoline into the drain of the catch basin 20-30 feet away to smoke out a coon. Mooch was to grab it as it ran out. They lit the gasoline---phoot---a small fire roared through the basin, blackened Mooch's face and arms, singed off his eyebrows, eyelashes and hair. And, NO COON! They sneaked him into his house to trim up his burnt hair and clean him up. Needless to say, the Moms didn't buy any of their explanations.

When he was about 12 he learned to drive cars which Gwynn's friends had parked in the street while they played bridge inside the home in the evenings, leaving the keys in their cars. He thinks they never knew, as he didn't turn on the lights until he had left the area. The cars were an old Essex, a Buick with a reverse shift, and a Model A Ford.

Saturday and Wednesday evenings stores stayed open until the farmers went home. Townspeople and farmers from the surrounding area came to town, bringing milk and eggs to the local cream stations. They took the money they received and bought groceries and supplies for the coming days. The poolroom (Bugs' Pool Hall) along with the bench outside it, and the movie house were kept busy.

Beer gardens, cafes, the barber shop, the dime store, variety stores, grocery stores, furniture stores and filling stations did a good business. There was a lot of foot traffic on Main and Second streets. Farm and local kids congregated in front of the stores, went to the movies, and just walked along the sidewalks. Traffic was heavy--including "Gloves" Neville, who drove continuously up and down the streets, making U turns, provoking yells from the kids.

People visited with friends and neighbors on the streets and in the stores. There was a variety of cars parked in the angled spaces in front of the store fronts, cars of all vintages and models of the time, and some owners and friends sat in them, visiting and watching all that was going on. What young boy would want to miss any of this?

John told me that one man tried and tried, engine roaring, to back out of a parking space and couldn't because some boys had "jacked up" his car, so that when he put it in gear it wouldn't move. A man named Joe, who was deaf, never heard his horn honk when the kids sat on his fender and lifted the externally mounted horn that had a short in it. Joe, in the meantime, sat behind the wheel unaware of what was taking place, waving at the laughing crowd around him.

Some of the drivers never looked back as they slowly backed out; there were several accidents, although no one was ever hurt; most people were aware of these things and were careful wherever they chose to walk.

One day a man named Lowell had been out hunting and got a ride home in the back seat in his friend Gene's car. His shotgun was lying across his lap (he didn't have the safety lock on) when the car hit a large hole in the roadway. The gun went off. The passenger in the front seat later told the story. "I heard a big bong and I turned around and shouted: 'Yene, vot the hell vas that?' Lowell yelled to the driver: 'Yene, I yust shot a big hole through yor car dor'." How lucky was that?

It was a gentle time--no one got mad, no one sued, everyone just laughed at and with each other, even if the joke was on them.

When he was about eleven or twelve he got a job of throwing the Des Moines Register and Tribune daily newspapers in town as he rode his bike, or walked in the winter snows; he also had to collect for these papers, 50 cents per week. One winter he also had five customers for the Omaha Bee.

He and all the Des Moines Register and Tribune paper carriers in the state of Iowa were assembled later for a group picture to be published in the brown section of the paper. They were taken by train to Des Moines for a day for a carriers' convention at the YMCA where they were entertained. Personal appearances and autograph signing by Nile Kinnick, All-American football player and Heisman trophy winner from the University of Iowa, and Coach Eddie Anderson, were highlights of their trip.

His most painful accident growing up happened one evening after dark as he rode his bike home with his hands draped over the handlebars and just happened to look up into an upstairs window where a young lady was undressing. He didn't see the pickup truck just in front of him and somersaulted over the handlebars into the bed of the pickup, resulting in a broken bone in his left hand.

When they were a little older, John and his friends pooled their little bit of money and bought an old car, a 1927 Ajax. This car they normally would push a block and ride a block; when the gasoline ran out of the vacuum tank (which was about a quart), they had to refill it--one quart at a time! The purpose of the vacuum pump was to draw gasoline from the gas tank to the motor; however, it never worked. Therefore, ride a block and push a block. Sometimes, for their gasoline supply, after the filling stations had closed for the night, they would go through and drain the pump hoses for excess gasoline.

In addition to the many other farms on the land around the area that are covered with crops and animals--most often cattle, dairy cows and swine--the Adams Family Ranch was a well-known farm of ten to eleven sections of land located just south of Odebolt.

The ranch was a beautiful place for many, many years, with several large white houses, barns, silos, and outbuildings. There were big trees outlining the perimeter and the roads criss-crossing property, which was well-tended and covered with crops of all kinds, mostly grain and tall, tall corn. There was a swimming pool, a water tower and a bunkhouse.

The Adams family had many hired hands; John and other young men in and around Odebolt worked there at harvest time when they were old enough. Men from the towns and country all around there rode into Odebolt in the freight train cars, and during the depression men came from many states looking for work or a handout of food, old clothes, etc. They marked with their own code the houses where they were able to get food and help; this was a clue to help the next men who came through.

The farm had many steam tractors, lots of machinery and farm equipment of all kinds, together with many beautiful show horses and over 100 mules. They had show horse stables and a large mule barn. The Adams family was highly respected in the community. It is heartbreaking now to see the farm so run-down. Much of the land has been divided into acreages which are owned by various people; the beautiful old houses, barns, stables, etc. were neglected for many years and many torn down.

There weren't any city or school buses in Odebolt, neither to grade school nor to the high school. Children that couldn't walk to school were driven every day, even from the farms around there. There were a few carpools for farm kids, although they weren't called that then.

Local people volunteered to drive the high school band and athletic teams to games, tournaments and other events and contests. The superintendent, coaches, teachers, school board members and parents piled the young people (each responsible for his own musical instrument, uniform, game equipment) into their 1931 Buicks, 1937, 1938 and 1939 Fords and other sedans. Cheerleaders went to the Sac County tournaments; the band performed only at home, except for the band tournaments held in other towns.

Their football games were played in the afternoon and at night. At football practice, one of John's classmates, a good friend, was quite a bit taller and larger than the others. His name was Sylvester "Luke" Lunkenheimer. The coach loaded him up with extra padding all around and used him for a blocking dummy. He was so strong that he tossed everybody around with ease. The fields had lights and they played with white footballs at night that could be seen more easily. There were no javelins used in their track meets--they used footballs for greater safety.

John graduated from high school in 1942 and went into the Army Air Corps. It was when he and some of his buddies came home after WW2 that they decided to come to Chillicothe Business College (CBC) and take advantage of the GI Bill (the government's funding of their schooling). Some of the returning young men majored in telegraphy and went to work for the railroad companies after graduation. John took the business course. He took a part-time janitorial job at the college to help out with fun expenses, and I helped him some with the cleaning--CBC is where we met.

He played on the Chillicothe Dux football and basketball teams with many other vets who had decided to attend that school, and their OLD gold-colored scratchy woolen basketball uniforms and high top shoes were a sight to behold! They traveled to many other towns to play, and, as a cheerleader, I was privileged to go, too.

At one of the away games, the guy that played the bass drum couldn't make it, and I was allowed to do it. I could at least keep the beat, and it was great fun twirling the "beaters" around above my head. We met so many fun people at that school in Chillicothe and are still friends with them, visiting occasionally. For a few years we had reunions, but, sadly many have since died.

As do other small towns around them, Odebolt has its town reunion, which is called "Creek Days", every summer. Souvenirs such as yearbooks, yearly tee shirts with logos, greeting cards with pictures of the old buildings, and other mementos are available. Nearby streets are closed off. Games and contests are held for kids and young people. There is always a big parade downtown with floats, marching bands and cheerleaders, big and bigger tractors and semi trucks, farm machinery, saddle horses, Shriners' small cars, etc., and wrapped hard candy is tossed from the floats to the people lined up watching.

Each graduating class has its own reunion at the same time. John sees many of his old friends there from all years, but each year many of them have passed away. We visit the graveyard where his mother, father and sister are buried every chance we get and he remembers the good times he had in his home town.

The school has been incorporated into others; the town has gradually lost most of its commercial business to surrounding larger towns and some of the downtown buildings have been torn down. It is now mostly a residential community. The creek running through Odebolt has been deepened and has memorial stones embedded along its banks, and well-kept park and picnic areas are available. It is fun to visit there and John enjoys going back every year and seeing old friends although there are fewer and fewer of them now.